THE GOSPEL

ACCORDING

TO US

THE GOSPEL ACCORDING TO *US*

On the Relationship Between Jesus and Christianity

by

DUNCAN HOLCOMB

Cross Cultural Publications, Inc.

CrossRoads Books

Cover Design by Chris Walker

Published by **CROSS CULTURAL PUBLICATIONS, INC.**
CROSS ROADS BOOKS
Post Office Box 506
Notre Dame, Indiana, 46556, U.S.A.
Phone: (219) 273-6526, 1-800-561-6526
FAX: (219) 273-5973

ISBN: 0-940121-38-7
Library of Congress Catalog Card Number: 96-86216

For Bill Hudson

ACKNOWLEDGMENTS

This is a work of crass plagiarism — there's hardly a phrase or idea in it that I haven't stolen outright from a book or a teacher or a friend. So it seems a bit silly to acknowledge a small portion of them now. The books are too many to name, even if I could remember them all. But I want to thank a number of wonderful people whose advice and encouragement over the five-year period this book was written helped make it possible. These include Royal Rhodes, Polly Robb, Chris Walker, Dave de Salvo, Louise Howlett, Gail Williams, Paul Nielsen, Eric Shaw, Hall Gardner, and Dave Walker. Special thanks are due to my father, Bill Holcomb, who always took the time to talk with me about issues of life and faith. I would not have developed an interest in theology without his direction, or accomplished much of anything without his remarkable example. Many heartfelt thanks to the Robb family for their love and support and the use of all their major household appliances. To my doppelganger, Tom Weathington, I owe a great debt; we should all have someone of his spirit and intellect to bounce ideas off of. At a low point in my work on this book I found new inspiration in David McCracken's *The Scandal of the Gospels* (Oxford), and he has since become a good friend and advisor. I strongly recommend *Scandal* for anyone who would like to look more closely into the way that scandal operates through the gospel narratives. To the brilliant New Testament scholar turned English country parson, Arthur Moore, many thanks, for his excellent advice, and for just being himself. Finally, to Bill Hudson, priest and friend. I like to think that this is the book Bill would have written if he'd lived long enough. But he asked too much of his heart, a mistake we'd all do well to make.

Birmingham   WDH
May 1996

The political and economic values of rational man are at bottom irrational ideologies, aimin g to achieve on earth a perfection which is only to be found in the beyond... thereby hopelessly confusing the values of both spheres. In this sense, all human values, no matter how real they seem to us, are unreal.

**Otto Rank, *Beyond Psychology*
New York: Dover Pubs 1958**

This people honors me only with lip service, while their hearts are far from me. Their reverence of me is worthless; the lessons they teach are nothing but human commandments.

**Isaiah 29:13
Mark 7:7**

**The chapter heading quotations are taken from
the prose and poetry of William Blake (1757-1827).**

FOREWORD

When I was a boy I loved stories. Stories of all kinds — those I read or saw on TV or heard from my parents or made up myself. Like most kids, my imaginative life was larger and fuller and more real than my material life, though at the time I didn't distinguish between the two. The world always consisted of a few small-town blocks, but they were immense and beautiful, and full with infinite possibility. I have gone back to visit those childhood homes once or twice. Each looks like a Lego miniature of my colossal past. As I've grown bigger my worlds have become smaller — both the material and the imaginative. I have learned to separate the two, and both have shrunk in the process.

I remember particularly well one building in a small town in northern Alabama where I once lived: the great brick edifice of the United Methodist Church. It seemed to four-foot me that nearly every brick in the state went into the making of that church. I used to stand with my back flush against its north wall and look straight up the bell tower until I was dizzy with a kind of reverse vertigo. The tower was perfectly square and straight and red as the soil it was built on, a stolid testament to the perfect geometry of life as I saw it. My own church building told me that God was old. The Methodist church told me that God was *great*. Today a Central Bank looms well over both.

The Methodists always hosted our town's Vacation Bible School, where every summer they gathered with the Presbyterians, Lutherans, Episcopalians, and a few stragglers from smaller Protestant churches outside of town. I loved that annual fortnight. Bible School was the one real event of my childhood summers, those stretching flatlands of time I secretly wished wouldn't last so long. That it was "religious" hardly occurred to me. VBS brought me together with my friends, gave us markers and construction paper and a comfortable place to sit. And it furnished us with wonderful and outrageous stories, from history, folk literature, and the Bible. Those tales were our earliest inspiration; they and drive-in movies peopled my imagination well into adolescence.

One VBS I remember particularly well, though for the anticipation more than the event. It had been announced in advance that that summer's program was going to kick off with a great movie, full of stars like John Wayne and Charlton Heston. It was called "The Greatest Story Ever Told." *The greatest story ever.* What could be better than that? My grade school associates and I soon called a colloquy to address the obvious question: which of our favorite stories would turn out to be "the greatest"? The debate was vigorous, even ugly, and we failed to reach a consensus, although a vocal minority averred that it would have something to do with the Green Berets. I'm sure I threw some of my own opinions around, though I don't remember what they were. I only remember feeling strangely miffed that someone had been granted the power to resolve such a momentous question in the first place. Who made this decision? And why *him*? I geared up for the film by preparing to be outraged at the choice, already a seasoned critic (a bad attitude and nearly broke) in fourth grade.

When the second Monday in July finally arrived, and they lowered the blinds in a hall that was already stifling and stagnant on that Alabama morning, I wasn't outraged. But I was disappointed. I knew *that* story already. It was not, in my ten-year-old opinion, the greatest story ever. The movie's setting, those great deserts and high plateaus on which it all took place, certainly impressed me. The miracles, too, were kind of interesting, and the crucifixion was gruesome and dramatic. But the preachy stuff in the middle took up most of the movie. The pace was oh so slow. And at the end, in spite of the presence of

God himself, the Romans were still in control!

The Greatest Story Ever Told ran at best a distant third, I decided, to King Arthur and Robin Hood. *Those* were real stories. The simple country boy who sets himself against the powers that be and all their unjust laws, who cares for the poor, the outcast and orphaned. With a band of rag-tag comrades he wanders through his homeland, performing deeds of miraculous skill and perception, working his will until the good king returns to rule again. And the rightful king, born a peasant, who is divinely commissioned at a lake and then goes about the kingdom with his devoted followers, doing good and overcoming evil through the strength of his moral code. He is eventually betrayed by those closest to him, but promises to return again, in the darkest hour of his people, with power and great glory. Those, I thought, were the greatest stories ever told. And of course I was right. It was just a long time before I realized that, like the plot of that old movie, I'd heard them before.

All the same, I learned a valuable lesson in Vacation Bible School that day, one I've held as divine truth ever since: read the book before you see the film. A book will sometimes ruin the movie for you, but the movie almost always ruins the book. If you've seen the movie already you're forever stuck with the visual images it provides, and these will dog you like a tired prejudice. But without them your mind will move about freely, interacting with the narrative, stimulated and inspired by it to create a lively world that is yours alone. Written tales, and spoken ones too, prompt an effort of child-like imagination that re-enactments don't, and the effect of this can't be overestimated. Robin Hood I knew from Howard Pyle rather than David Selznick, and Robin struck me as a man of great purpose and vision. But Jesus did not. Many years went by before I began to give the man from Galilee the attention I had lavished on the one from Sherwood. That is: before I began to read about him.

It may seem strange that someone could grow up in a family of Christians, attend a Christian church in a Christian nation, and not read even one of the four accounts of the life and work of Jesus of Nazareth that appear in the New Testament. But that's what happened. And it certainly seems strange to me now that someone who scoured his local library for good stories would ignore one on the shelf next to his bed. It just never occurred to me to sit and read a gospel narrative as I had almost every other narrative that passed before my eyes.

Why not? There are a number of possible reasons. For starters, I never saw others sit and read the gospels as they did other books. You may have entertained an opinion about the Bible, or owned a good number of them, or carried one to church every Sunday, or pondered a passage from it every night before going to sleep. But you didn't sit and read a book from it. From early in life I intuited that you don't just read the Bible. It must *mean* something. The fact of reading, and the context in which the reading was done, and the type of person doing the reading, were at least as important as the reading itself. If you were a young boy, for instance, spending time with "The Good Book" meant either that you had a vocation for the ministry, or that you were what some folks called a "morbid child."

Another reason: it seemed to me that you *read* books, but that you *study* scripture (and "study" was not a thing I did with my free time). The Elizabethan language of our Bibles contributed mightily to that understanding. You needed to join a study group to read the Bible properly; you bought commentaries and devotional tracts. As I grew older I tended to equate Biblical literature with that of Shakespeare — beautiful, and "good for you" in some vague way, but tough to get through. (Was it Hamlet who said "Sufficient unto the day are the troubles thereof"?) There were other, more personal factors at work, and probably some I'm not aware of. But whatever the reasons, for better or worse, from year to year, the black volume bound in ersatz leather sat on my bottom shelf next to the Golden Book Encyclopedia, and I knocked off forty-seven Hardy Boys in a row.

Still, in spite of all this, I always figured I knew about Jesus of Nazareth. After sixteen years of formal education, a dozen Vacation Bible Schools, a score of nativity and passion plays, one mediocre movie, and more than a few hundred church services, how could I not? And yet there was one thing lacking. Although I grew up in a religious town, with a Bible-to-Person ratio of at least four-to-one, and attended a church of the Protestant Reformation, a movement dedicated in part to proclaiming the primacy of sacred scriptures, I had managed never to read one — a scripture, that is. It was many years, and many miles removed from the place of my origins, before I first picked up a copy of the New Testament and began to read. A slow and sleety day in Connecticut; the Gospel of Mark.

Etymologists tell us that the old English word "gospel" means "good news." Good or not, Mark was certainly news to me. If not the greatest story ever told, it felt at the very least like a strange and unique one. By this time in my life I was a widely-read student of fiction and philosophy who could imagine nothing new under his literary sun. So Mark came as a surprise. It read like "a new thing," both in content and form: new wine in fresh skins, as Jesus himself puts it. And Jesus is the source of the novelty. As temple officers report to the chief priests, "No one has ever spoken like this man." Jesus speaks of "a new commandment" and covenant and way of living; he hints at "things hidden since the foundation of the world." And he seems to relish the response he gets to his novel themes and ideas. On one occasion Jesus gleefully notes to his audience that what he does and says "has indeed caught you unawares," a remark that at first blush seemed directed specifically at me. But in the gospels, I soon noticed, *all* of his listeners respond with shock and — one of the gospels' favorite words — "astonishment." "What is this?" a bewildered crowd exclaims early in Mark. "A new teaching!"

When I'd finished reading Mark I didn't feel that I had really grasped the nature of the man or his message. But there was "Good News," at least, in discovering that I wasn't alone. No one in the gospels, really *no one*, understands Jesus of Nazareth. "The rabble" and the Pharisees certainly don't: they expect him to lead an armed insurrection against Rome. His disciples, too, comprehend little of what he says, and second-guess much of what they do. Even his family is baffled, and often distressed by his behavior. They pressure him to leave the crowds and come home; on one occasion they even try to kidnap him! It turns out that "his own brothers did not believe in him" and that in Nazareth "they took offense at him" for his prophetic pretensions. "Where did he get all of this?" they protest. He is expelled from their synagogue, and then from the town, and nearly thrown off the hill it sits on. As his ministry grows increasingly sour and dangerous even his closest friends work against him. His right-hand man openly opposes him in the very moment he is made the head of his "church"; his own treasurer plots to sell him to the authorities. Jesus comes to express horror and dismay at the turn his ministry takes, and speaks of himself as one in the long line of hated and misunderstood and ill-fated prophetic truth-sayers who populate Israel's troubled history. "A prophet is not without honor," he remarks bitterly, "except in his own country, and among his own kin, and in his own house."

In my second reading of Mark this comment — just an aside, really — struck me more than anything else Jesus says. It seemed to be addressed somehow to the sense of strangeness and confusion that I, a cradle Christian, felt in reading the gospels for the first time. Here the disparity between what I'd been taught about Jesus, and what I was reading in the story before me, found a remarkable context. *Jesus himself anticipates it!* He even implies that it's inevitable. A true prophet by nature is heeded and honored, deferred to and considered carefully — except in his own house, even the house built for him, the seat of honor established in his name. I grew up in one of his houses, and what I read in the gospels was a surprise to me.

I was told that Jesus is both Christ and son of David. But I read of a peasant who questions how "the Christ" could possibly be David's son. I always thought that he promotes the institution of the family. But I read of a prophet who leaves his hometown, who never marries, who promises to bring disruption and discord to happy households. I understood Jesus to be meek and mild, pleasant, positive, and perfect. And I read of a young man who denies that he is good, who is capable of appalling anger and outrage, who is often tired and frustrated, who at the end of his life is overwhelmed with "terror and anguish." I was taught that Jesus blesses the nation that follows him. But I read of an Israelite who expresses only contempt for the impulses and devotions of nationalism. I always believed that he inspired the ethic of hard work and material acquisition that has helped make Western civilization so prosperous. But I read of a carpenter's son who is never seen working, who directs his followers to live from day to day like the birds and lilies "that neither toil nor spin." I read of a man who expresses disdain for established religion as he knows it, for many religious practices, and for all the religious types who populate the world in which he lives. And I always thought of Jesus of Nazareth as the founder of the world's largest religion.

This was an impressive list of misconceptions, but before I had finished Mark I'd already decided to think of myself as indicative of a trend rather than singularly stupid. That seemed like the most convenient tack at the time. And general ignorance about the gospels really was easy to find once I began to look for it. It's on display in newspapers and classrooms, legislatures and street corners, among the unschooled and the hyper-educated, zealous churchgoers and chronic atheists. Americans are a religious people. According to

George Gallup, more than nine out of ten American adults say they believe in God, and 86% profess that Jesus is his son. Yet only half of those surveyed could name one of the four gospels. Fewer than that could identify the preacher of the Sermon on the Mount.

Much of what people *do* claim to know about Jesus is simply wrong; misunderstandings range from the sublime to the hilarious. I offended a co-worker recently when I suggested that Jesus was Jewish. (She often professes to "love Jesus," but isn't much interested in discussing him.) Another acquaintance was surprised to hear that his last name was not "Christ." This is the Bible Belt, by the way. Maybe you've heard about the Alabama state senator's speech in opposition to bilingual education: "If English is good enough for Jesus Christ, it's good enough for me."

The exact causes of our confusion are hard to pin down, though suspects are plentiful. It may be true, as many say, that people don't read anymore, so that the gospel texts, as with other texts, are neglected in our post-literate culture. Of course, reading, reading well and closely, has always been hard work. But it can be especially difficult with books like those in the Bible, which we've heard so much about before we even learn the alphabet! We live in a nation that claims "the Bible" as its greatest inspirational text, a society packed with shared understandings about "what's in the Bible," a culture that relies on "the Bible" for its sense of special value and divine sanction and makes movies like "The Greatest Story Ever Told" so we don't bother reading the thing. We can all savor the lingering aromas of the gospel texts that have been kept brewing over the centuries, but many of us never bother to taste them for ourselves.

When we do decide to read the gospels we encounter many obstacles, real and imagined. The most common English translation, the one a novice is most likely to pick up, is written in an old English dialect that is truly remote from modern ears.

This in itself has proved too great an obstacle for some, and has led to all sorts of misreadings. (I once heard a harried mother of three ruefully quote Jesus' injunction to "suffer the little children.") The avalanche of biblical scholarship produced in this century has been just as forbidding. The works of form, source, and redaction criticism, the various feminist and reader-response and post-structural approaches to the gospel texts, have led many people to believe that the task of understanding much of anything in either Testament is beyond their untutored abilities. Certainly the "scope" of modern biblical criticism has brought the gospel texts into greater focus than ever before. But as a result they sometimes look just that much further away.

Public discourse about Jesus tends to be either shrill or absent, and usually the latter. Public speakers, in attempts to be inclusive, speak only of "God." Atheists generally refuse to express any interest in someone who has been worshipped as a deity. Christians tend to be defensive about the man they call Savior, and may refuse to discuss Jesus unconditionally with others, as if he might be damaged by honest consideration, or is somehow beyond it. The subject, when raised, seems to generate a singular awkwardness and discomfort in just about everyone. I remember watching a daytime talk show in which a "Grand Dragon" of the Ku Klux Klan sat in as guest. The voluble host was taking the usual pot shots at this widest of targets. How in the world were you raised, she asked? Didn't your mama teach you about right and wrong? The Dragon calmly replied that he had been raised in a family of deeply committed Christians. From them he had learned the value of racial segregation. Then he looked up into the audience and said that the world's single greatest advocate of segregation was Jesus Christ. At that the rhythm of the repartee was broken. The audience seemed to hold its breath, and the host with them. "So," she finally managed. "How long have you been a Klansman?"

The reasons for our neglect continue to multiply. Public

schools are prohibited by law from teaching about Jesus. This is a remarkable thing to consider, whether you condone it or not: the study of our culture's primary text has been partially banned by our culture. What we may learn about the Bible has to fit into one hour a week at best. If we don't get it there we may not get it at all. Even at many major colleges and universities you can't study the gospels — no such course is offered. They are routinely ignored by cultural historians, philosophers, and literary critics, considered by them to be somehow out of their purview. Philosophers arbitrarily label them as belonging to a different area of the human search for meaning. Historians won't touch a man almost entirely absent from surviving historical records. And after two thousand years we're only now beginning to explore the wealth of the gospels as literature. This avoidance by the intellectual community is a particularly curious thing, given the unique place of Jesus in western culture, and the profound influence of the gospels on its art and scholarship. But it's there for all to see.

Stranger still: neglect of the gospels is in evidence even among Christian theologians and popular religious writers, the liberal and conservative, the fundamentalist and evangelical. Many Christian social philosophers simply content themselves with a facile reflection on the greatness of Jesus' teachings as they move on to Paul, or the church fathers, or modern inspirational authors. A number of contemporary theologians argue that there can be "no gospel before the resurrection," a stance that manages to dispense with Jesus quite neatly. Haven't a staggering number and variety of books been written about this man, you ask? Oh yes. But most offer precious little in the way of careful consideration of his specific words, actions, and ideas. The most beloved and widely-read theologian of our time, C. S. Lewis, wrote a best-selling book designed to explain and defend the religion of Christianity. In it Jesus of Nazareth is *never quoted*. Like so many others, Lewis is interested in Jesus only as a metaphysical being. The words of the man who speaks in the gospels are dismissed with two astonishing sentences: "There has been no lack of good advice for the last four thousand years. A bit more makes no difference."[1]

A peculiar position, this one, for the most famous man in world history, and the four famous books about him. Sometimes it all looks like a great conspiracy of silence on behalf of left and right, old and young, religious and agnostic alike. Sometimes it looks like an oversight. But what makes the situation all the more suspicious is the fact that our great collusion itself is unremarked upon! Not only do we avoid coherent and comprehensive discussion of Jesus' teachings — we ignore the *fact* of that avoidance. Maybe there's more going on here than we're willing to acknowledge. Even if our neglect is unconscious, its prevalence suggests that we're up to something. What accounts for it all? Why do we avoid the gospels? Do they make themselves difficult to hear? Or are we just being obtuse?

In this short book I want to consider the reasons why we disregard or misunderstand the Jesus of Nazareth we meet in the gospels, and then reflect on some specific differences between his teachings and those of the church and the world. The book is organized into three sections. In the first section we'll look at the difficulties we encounter when reading the gospels. Chapter One addresses problems we have with their content, and Chapter Two looks at our problems with their form. The second section is devoted to the reaction of Jesus' contemporaries to his words and ideas. My feeling is that in our response to the gospels we can hear the echo of theirs. Chapter Three considers the disciples, and Chapter Four the Pharisees. Chapter Five then attempts to locate the fundamental source of our historic disagreement with Jesus. This leads into Section Three, in which we'll compare our most cherished values with his, as best we can understand them.

My hope is that through this kind of examination we can

---

[1] *Mere Christianity*; New York: Collier Books, 1952 p. 137

more openly confront and consider Jesus' teachings and his unique approach to life, much of which, even after two thousand years, still feels strangely new and disturbing. It makes no sense for us to choose our saviors by default, or based on old assumptions, hearsay, or millennia of time-worn tradition. We need to make a conscious choice about what, and who, we really want to believe.

PART I

I

SCANDAL AND OFFENSE

I am sure This Jesus will not do
Either for Englishman or Jew.

"The Everlasting Gospel"

AT THE BEGINNING of his gospel Luke remarks, almost apologetically, that "many have undertaken to compile a narrative of the things which have been accomplished among us." Imagine that — a mere generation removed from Jesus' death and the market is already glutted with books on the man! Most of those apparently didn't make it past their first run, since they haven't survived through to today. I can only speculate as to what some of them were like. *Jesus: The Untold Story. Jesus Dearest.* Maybe not unlike many of the books written on him today.

I would dearly love to show Luke around the shelves of my local bookstore. Even he would be amazed to see the number and variety of books on his Galilean, and the claims they make about him. Once I had read all four gospels for the first time I went there in search of other accounts of his life, and discovered much more than I expected. I found a book titled *Jesus the Magician.* I found another called *Jesus the Anarchist.* I had a look through *Jesus: The First Human Behaviorist, Jesus: The Ultimate ET,* and *Jesus is a Special Person.* Some of the books simply touted fun new theories, like *Jesus Lived In India.* Quite a few made great claims on the truth designed to set us free. There was *Jesus: His Last Will and Testament,* for example. There were *two* books bearing the delicious title of *The Gospel According to Jesus.* That was too hard to pass up: I grabbed the first one and turned to its introduction.

The author seemed to take Luke's opening comment as an implied challenge. Why write yet another narrative of the life and death of Jesus of Nazareth? His answer was plain. Jesus has long been obscured and distorted, by the gospel writers who first characterized him, and by the church that made him its own. His gentle image has been sullied by many of the terrible words and ideas ascribed to him, and his mystical vision subverted to meet the needs of his first followers. The task at hand, as the author described it, was to sift through these early texts to uncover the *real* Jesus, a man who is not quite the one we know from Matthew *et al.*

The real Jesus: just the person I was looking for! "Obscured and distorted" pretty well summed up my first foggy feelings on the issue. I bought the book and took it home, inspired by the author's earnest spirit and energy. He had a keen ear for the kind of language and forms of expression Jesus uses. He knew something about the character and habits of the people of first-century Palestine. And he clearly wanted to be faithful to the spirit of his unique subject, Jesus of Nazareth. As chapter followed chapter, a vivid portrait of a very interesting man slowly came into focus. He had been a precocious child, always interested in religious issues, though certainly no conformist. Actually, he was a bit of a radical and mystic, very much up on the popular philosophies of his day. And as he grew he refined for himself a beautiful vision of the world, a vision he wanted to share with all peoples, regardless of race or creed.

You guessed it. The portrait was of the author himself, a man busy at work behind his hand-crafted narrative, emphasizing the things in Jesus' life and work that he saw as profound and inspiring, and deleting whatever seemed unbelievable, or illiberal, or out of kilter with his own mystical philosophy. Healings he liked, feedings he didn't. Apocalyptic renewal made the final cut, apocalyptic judgment did not. Jesus eating, drinking, crying, praying, suffering, all remained. But his bold statements about being the savior of the world? His hard words of condemnation and abuse? Gone.

Nothing in his portrait was an outright deception. All this latest redactor really did was to highlight his favorite features of Jesus, in the same harmless way we keep flattering pictures of ourselves and our friends and discard the others. You see, he couldn't possibly revere a man, or a god, whom he dislikes. (Could you?) So his decision was a propitious one. It's nearly impossible to explain away all the difficult and discomfiting elements of Jesus' character. Better by far to take out the offensive stuff entirely by claiming that it's inauthentic.

Still, the product of this revision was not what you might expect. Although the expurgated Jesus that remained was certainly admirable, even inspired, it seemed to me that something special about him had been lost. One of Jesus' most striking attributes is his penchant for preaching the hard word, doing what is supremely unpopular, steadfastly refusing to perform, pander, or placate. His unpredictable behavior and lack of concern for his popularity are part of what make him such an intriguing and estimable man. These features even seem to attract more people to Jesus, at least at first. In this context it's hard to say that even his most offensive saying is not really his ("anyone who blasphemes against the Holy Spirit will never be forgiven"), or that what such a thing might mean could not be a valuable subject for discussion.

As its author himself notes, *The Gospel According to Jesus* is not the first effort of its kind. It's the same book that has been written, again and again, since the original gospels were circulated. The first edition appeared way back in the second century, when a Greek gnostic named Marcion decided to reshape Christian scripture into what he thought should be its true and eternal form, the one he said Jesus really intended.

Since then the work has gone on without interruption; its list of credits, from Tatian to Tolstoy, is truly astonishing. Even Thomas Jefferson tried his hand at revising the gospels to his liking. The noblest man of the Enlightenment found it impossible to believe that "such contradictions should have proceeded from the same being," and he set out with a pair of scissors to resolve them. Jefferson's *Life and Morals of Jesus of Nazareth* was eventually published by his family and distributed to the members of Congress. Most recently a convocation of more than one hundred American gospel scholars conducted what came to be dubbed "The Jesus Seminar." With colored beads they voted on the likelihood that individual slices of gospel called "pericopes" were actually spoken by Jesus (most likely sayings get a red bead, less likely a pink, then gray, and so on). When they finished the scholars published a color-coded gospels. Would it surprise you to hear that nearly half of Jesus' words appear in black?

Now the wide differences in doctrine and methodology over the last two thousand years do serve to distinguish all these many revisions of the gospels from one another. But it's important to note that all share one central feature: all work to present their audience with a more palatable Jesus, a milder man, a little more politic, someone less abrasive and obtuse than the one we encounter in Luke, Mark, Matthew, and John. To a great extent our history of reading and translating and re-writing the gospels has been the history of avoiding much of what Jesus does and says, simply because we find it troubling. "It's not the parts of the Bible I don't understand that bother me," Mark Twain once wrote. "It's the parts I *do* understand." This pretty well sums up what both scholars and lay people often feel when faced with the gospels, but would never allow themselves to say. It's the key to our misapprehension of Jesus' teachings, helping to explain why we manage not to read them too closely, even to avoid many parts completely: we find them *offensive*. Jesus himself suggests this as the reason. "Why do you not understand what I say?" he asks an uneasy crowd, and then answers his own question. "It is because you cannot bear to hear my word."

The more I look for examples of this the more it seems to be the organizing principle of every approach to the gospels, Christian or agnostic, liberal or conservative, ancient or modern. The end results are always somewhat different, of course, because different groups and ages finds different things offensive, but the hermeneutic remains the same (*hermeneutics: the study of principles of interpretation*). Consider for example the Common Lectionary, the guidebook of what is read and not read in most Christians churches every Sunday. It excludes many of the most difficult, painful, and offensive Bible passages from its list of weekly readings. The gospels, in particular, are sanitized for our protection. Even when a section is judged acceptable by its standards sometimes a half-verse is left out here or there, or a dialogue stopped early, to smooth over the rough spots. And historical criticism of the gospels effortlessly mops up whatever problems remain. If a passage read in church feels too harsh or uncompromising we can still rest easy, knowing that a majority of scholars have already dismissed it with a wave of the pen as words put in gentle Jesus' mouth by somebody else.

This is a universal tendency, and it has gone largely unnoted. One of the first and only to address it was the beatific English poet and engraver William Blake. Blake dubbed "Creeping Jesus" the tepid, flabby moralist whom he said had replaced the unusual and often difficult man we encounter in the gospels. In his brilliant lyric ballad "The Everlasting Gospel" Blake summoned all the power of his art and rhetoric to challenge this symbol of "sneaking submission" and compare him to the man who

> *scorn'd Earth's parents, scorn'd Earth's God*
> *And mock'd the one and the other's Rod*

But Blake, like his favorite subject, was ignored or misunderstood by his contemporaries, and died in near obscurity. "The Everlasting Gospel" remained hidden in his notebooks for generations, and Creeping Jesus is more popular in our own hyper-sensitive day than ever before.

◆   ◆   ◆

What is the approach taken by Jesus himself, and by the gospel writers? Not quite the same. They refuse to deny or moderate the offensiveness of their narratives. (*Why* is a question we're not yet ready to consider.) In fact, in blank contrast to posterity, they make "offense" a central theme. *Skandalon* and *proskomma* are among the most commonly used words in the four gospels. The verb form is usually translated "offend." The noun appears most often as "trap," "snare," and "stumbling block." They are spoken by Peter, Satan, the disciples, and others. They're used consistently by the narrators, who go to some lengths to point out how indecent and insulting Jesus' words often sound to his listeners. But the two words are used most by Jesus, who is well aware of the essential offensiveness of much of what he says and does. In fact he publicly acknowledges how difficult and painful his words can be — he pronounces "blessed" all those who merely "take no offense at me." A telling beatitude, that one.

Almost everything Jesus says and does challenges what people, the poor and the wealthy, Gentile and Jew, believe to be valuable and important. "As Jonah was to the Ninevites," he promises, "so will the Son of Man be to this generation." And so he is. Long-reverenced law and custom, social organization, hallowed religious teaching, simple common sense, even basic standards of decorum and hygiene are called into question. "Let *these* words sink into your ears" he challenges his audience on more than one occasion, flaunting their hardness. He tells one young man to give away everything he owns, and counsels another not to bother burying his father. He recommends offering aid and comfort to Roman soldiers, and announces plans to tear down the Temple in Jerusalem. He suggests that people offer their faces to be struck. He equates lustful looks with adultery. He condemns outright the common practice of divorce. He insists that a man should "hate father and mother, wife and children, brothers and sisters, even his own life," but love his enemies. Jesus sums it up best himself: "I tell you these words of scripture are destined to be fulfilled in me: 'He was counted as one of the rebellious'."

It's little wonder that the men and women listening to Jesus rarely reply to his pronouncements — they're probably trying to get their breath back. ("He has a demon" is one of the few comments mustered in response.) Some, like the Pharisees, or the rich young man, can't help but take it all to heart, and they walk away worse for their encounter. The disciples are certainly put off by much of what he says, and eventually take to challenging it. "This is a hard saying," they complain more than once. "Who can listen to it?" Even Jesus' family and friends are shocked and angered. In his home town, we're told, the locals very nearly throw him off a cliff.

Not everyone reacts this way, though. There are others in the gospels, like Jesus' mother, and the Samaritan woman at Jacob's well, who manage not to be put off by what sound like personal affronts. Somehow they digest it all, without denying the offensiveness, and even express a measure of devotion to their offender. Still others we never hear about. The gospels don't provide us with a reaction from Martha, for instance, or Nicodemus, to Jesus' tough and challenging words. The conversation is held, the words and ideas exchanged, and the narrative moves on, so that the reader is left with his or her own undigested response — suspended, like the grumbling workers in that parabolic vineyard, in the moment of collision.

Here is a crucial point. It's a defining characteristic of the gospel texts, and a testament to their storytelling skill, that

Jesus' offensive words and actions don't strike us as static moments in history, mercifully buffered by time. Because they're narratives, and because the careful reader lives through each narrative moment, the gospels convey a double offense — first to the people in the gospels who meet and hear Jesus, and then to the reader of those gospels. That offense is lived and experienced fresh by everyone in every age who picks up these texts and reads.

It's equally characteristic of the gospels that *no one* escapes unscandalized. Jesus manages to spread his effrontery across a broad range of peoples and ideologies. He's tough on both the religious and the profane, a burr in the sandal of rationalist and mystic alike. He's too unkempt and iconoclastic for conservatives, too strict and impolitic for liberals, too idealistic for pragmatists, too vital for the pious. Sometimes the man is just abrasive or obtuse — hard where you might want him to be gentle and yielding where you hope he'd be stalwart, kind to prostitutes and tough on his mother, restrained before Pilate and impulsive with a fig tree. At other times he's a legitimate metaphysical problem. He offends some by claiming to be God, or Son of God, and doing supernatural things. He offends others by claiming to be Man, or Son of Man, and doing natural things.

This hasn't discouraged a garden variety of causes and ideologies from trying to claim Jesus as their own, of course, and this can be done by keeping to generally accepted understandings about "the Christ." The religious left and the religious right, for example, are equally sure that they have Jesus firmly and exclusively in their ideological camp. The right sees in him an advocate of traditional morality; the left sees a patron of social welfare and political liberalism. But problems arise when they encounter the gospels. There Jesus offends both groups in equal measure.

Let's consider a specific issue to illustrate this point: Jesus' attitude and behavior toward women. The gospel writers openly present what in some early Christian circles was already considered something of a scandal — the single man Jesus and his coterie of female followers. Women would make any itinerant religious group look more or less like a commune, or a Gypsy band, or worse. But they are included, without shame or explanation. In fact, they're key members of Jesus' following. It is the women who provide for the group "out of their own means." Jesus speaks to them openly and individually, disregarding the Jewish convention regarding their supposed inferiority and ritual "uncleanness." This bachelor even heals a woman suffering from hemorrhages. In one remarkable scene he allows a woman whose sins are well known to anoint his head with oil, wipe his feet with her hair, kiss them again and again, and rub them with ointment from an alabaster jar. (Picture *that*.) He is particularly close to a woman from Magdala, a notorious town on the northwest coast of the Sea of Galilee. Yet another Mary, the sister of Lazarus, is close to him too. And there is Martha and Salome and Susanna and Joanna (the wife of Herod's steward!). Jesus lives with them all, and never marries — precisely the kind of arrangement many religious groups have always condemned as immoral. This mix of the low and corrupt and criminal and outcast is the last one most of us who call ourselves Christians would want to claim as our own, but it's the only group to which Jesus ever belongs.

There is plenty in that to offend the conservative mind; there is just as much to scandalize the liberal. In his treatment of women Jesus sometimes appears openly sexist (as well as racist and ageist). He chooses only men, only young Jewish men, as his twelve apostles. The women, for their part, seem to perform most of the domestic and menial work for the community of believers, an arrangement Jesus never questions. In fact it has often been argued by critics of the gospels that Jesus' teachings implicitly support social and sexual inequality. He teaches that the last shall be first, that it's more blessed to serve, that the meek will inherit the earth. Never once does he suggest that the "oppressed," "those who mourn," "who hunger and thirst for righteousness" object to the sorry conditions under which they live. Never once does he tell them to fight the social and economic institutions that perpetuate those conditions. For many liberals this is a "slave morality," designed precisely to keep women and children and the poor and outcast in their place by making them believe they're somehow blessed in their present oppressed condition.

I myself am a natural-born liberal, more sensitive to offense than I'd like to be, but proud of my convictions. And when I began to read the gospels I certainly found plenty to upset me. I remember being especially bothered by the scene in which Jesus is accosted by a Canaanite woman whose child is possessed. It's a distressing and poignant moment, one of the starkest ever committed to prose. This woman apparently knows the brashness of what she does in speaking to a Jewish holy man, she a female and a Palestinian. She even points out both key differences in calling Jesus "Son of David." Jesus speaks "not a word" to her in response, but the woman is desperate. She continues to shout after him, imploring him for help, like the parabolic widow before an unjust judge. Even then only the disciples are affected by her constant pleadings, and they insist that Jesus deal with her. Finally he does, picking up on her "Son of David" epithet by saying that he was sent to "the lost sheep of the House of Israel." This stiff refusal the woman somehow takes as an opportunity. She kneels before Jesus and speaks a perfect prayer: "Lord, help me." Then he, unaccountably, and most offensively, replies that it is not fair to "take the children's food and throw it to the dogs."

This is certainly "a hard saying." Who can listen to it? As with all of Jesus' offensive words, it's hard for the person in the gospel story to whom it is spoken, and for the reader of the gospel itself. It certainly upset and angered me — for a liberal there is no baser comment than a racist one. I am not alone. The encounter is left out of almost every gospel rewrite, constituting as it has an occasion of some embarrassment. The "to the dogs" line most biblical exegetes refuse to admit as belonging to Jesus. They claim that he could not possibly have made a remark that intolerant, that racist, that offensive.

For the Canaanite woman, however, Jesus' remark is an occasion for faith. It would have been brave enough of her to ignore the hurtful words and continue pleading on behalf of her dying child. But, amazingly, she accepts Jesus' chosen image of her as "dog," even takes and builds on it: "Ah yes, Lord, but even the dogs eat scraps that fall from their masters' table." Jesus stops, and marvels at this. The one is indeed "blessed... who takes no offense" at him — the woman's daughter is healed. (This was a satisfactory resolution for her, but not for me, since I found supernatural events offensive too.)

That scene is still hard for me to deal with, and always will be. In a petty way I console myself with what conservatives have to confront in the gospels. Their row may be even harder to hoe, given what they have at stake in "The Bible." Jesus has long been held up by conservatives as the central advocate of traditional Western morality, which emphasizes the value of hard work, the importance of respecting authority, the sacredness of the family. I am too much my parents' child to attack these standards; my only question is whether the Jesus of the four gospels supports them. Working hard, respecting authority — these are not exactly his strong points. Let's try "the sacredness of the family" instead. That's a sure thing, isn't it? Driving past a church in my neighborhood recently I noticed a huge banner that read "Jesus Supports the Family." In our culture this assertion is considered not only true, but a truism.

To give conservative interpretation every leeway let's put aside as prophetic rhetoric Jesus' brash statements about the importance of hating father and mother, or his wanting to set family members against each other so that "a man's foes will be those of his own household." That Jesus himself never marries, even though he surrounds himself with women, let's attribute to the singularity of his calling. Rather than be bothered by all the people who abandon their families, leave relations untended or unburied on his instruction, let's take the way Jesus acts toward his own family as the measure of his feelings on this issue.

The stories are presented in the gospels without explanation or attenuation; they are blunt at best. On an early family trip to Jerusalem for Passover Jesus wanders off for three days. After looking all over the city Mary finally finds him in the Temple. The precocious boy is standing on his own amongst his elders, listening and being heard. Mary, greatly relieved to have found her first-born son, enters and says "Your father and I have been looking for you anxiously." Jesus replies crisply that she should have known he would be in "*my* father's house." This kind of scene is not uncommon. When his ministry gains momentum it becomes impossible for his family to get near him. On one occasion they are blocked by a crowd from seeing him and send word of their arrival. Jesus' response is sharper than a serpent's tooth: "Who are my mother and my brothers?" Apparently they go away without getting even a glimpse of him. Eventually his family become so distraught that they try to kidnap him (no details are provided). But Jesus isn't anxious to return to a town where once he was very nearly killed, or to a household where even "his own brothers did not believe in him."

Perhaps you will say that even this is not a fair indicator. After all, Joseph really isn't Jesus' father, and his siblings are only half-relations. But this gets us into deeper trouble, since Jesus' biological relationship to his family is itself a source of scandal and offense. It's not surprising that a Jewish tradition developed in the first centuries of the Christian era that Jesus was Mary's illegitimate son. Jesus is the first of at least five boys and two girls in the household, but his relationship to Joseph is left murky at best. If Joseph is Jesus' biological father then Jesus is a member of the House of David (tribe of Judah). Mary, however, is a kinswoman of Elizabeth, a "daughter of Aaron" (the priestly tribe of Levi). So to which tribe does Jesus belong, that of his putative father or of his biological mother? In other words, is he priest or son of David? Or somehow both? If he's not physically related to Joseph it's hard to see how he is "of the house and lineage of David." And a Jewish man's lineage doesn't descend from his mother. Early in his life people refer to Jesus as "the son of Mary," a suspicious phrase for a patriarchal and patrilineal society like that of the Jews. It wouldn't normally be used even if Joseph had died in Jesus' infancy. Some have argued that when a group of Pharisees remark to Jesus "*We* were not born of fornication," they are implying something very specific. Now this is head-strong reading (and would an illegitimate child be presented at the Temple?). But even unfounded rumors of illegitimacy are offensive to Christians, an offense the gospels nurture as much as they squelch.

Jesus himself carefully avoids these questions, uncomfortable with biological ties, almost envious of the eunuchs, whom he equates with angels. Consider what he says to and about his mother, a woman sometimes worshipped as a deity in her own right: he goes to some lengths to dissociate himself from her. Not until his death is near do we even hear him call Mary "mother," and only then to make her "mother" to another man. At a wedding feast in Cana, when Mary approaches him about getting more wine, Jesus replies with the painfully curt "Woman, what have you to do with me?" His response is not really about the wine at all — it's about the relationship between the two that lets her make the request in the first place. Remember the scene in which Jesus is traveling along a road, accompanied by a large crowd of followers. An anonymous woman shouts out the first *Ave*: "Blessed is the womb that bore you, and the breasts that you sucked!" Jesus shouts back: "Blessed rather are those who hear the word of God and keep it!"

Now a great deal can and should be said in response to this.

One is that Mary herself doesn't take offense at what Jesus says. She continues to follow and support this most difficult of sons throughout his life, even to the cross, which is more than the disciples can say. After Jesus rebukes her at Cana she quietly goes to the servants and tells them to "do whatever he says" — an almost miraculously measured response (and a miracle is exactly what she gets). Mary's influence on Jesus is an implicit one, evident mostly in the strong relationships he develops with other women. It may be no coincidence that Jesus' closest female companion is another woman named Mary, and she too a woman who once suffered a "reputation." Mary's devotion to Jesus in spite of everything she endures is a moving testament to the unconditional love of motherhood: unconditional love is what Jesus grows up to teach.

Still, it's nearly impossible to explain away all of Jesus' words about families, or his attitude toward his own. The best religious and political conservatives can do is ignore them, and all "dysfunctional" families in the Bible, starting with Adam and Eve's, and rely on a few passages from Deuteronomy or Romans to defend their social agenda. The liberals, for their part, avoid Jesus' reference to God in masculine terms like "Father" and "Lord" by writing gospels according to them where he prays to "Our Father-Mother in heaven." Remember, the scandal of the gospels is not static; each succeeding age finds things about Jesus that insult its most sacred sensibilities. And, in every age, these things are put aside. The offense is too hard to face in the courageous way Mary does; we've decided instead to ignore it altogether.

II

BRIDEGROOMS AND LANDFILLS

*The Beauty of the Bible is that the most
Ignorant & Simple Minds understand it Best.*

Blake's Annotations to Thornton's
"New Translation of the Lord's Prayer""

WHEN I TURNED twenty-five I decided to address my closet
fascination with the gospels and enrolled in the graduate
program of Religious Studies at the University of Virginia. It
was a furtive move at best. It has always seemed to me that an
interest in theology is like an interest in, say, philology; I was
strangely loath to tell anyone about it. People tend to think of
the more obscure academic pursuits as valuable in some vague
way, but rather quaint, even suspicious or, worse yet, *admirable.*
But I never felt any vocation for the ministry, and no particular
spur other than idle curiosity. So once the decision was made I
began to work the best angles, to stress the youthful
impracticality of my move, the impetuous fling of an unbridled
mind, and this helped take the edge off such an apparently
earnest endeavor.

My graduate advisor that first year was Dr. Nathan Scott,
the well-published literary scholar and priest. Dr. Scott, black,
older, a bit cranky, and wonderfully erudite, had become a
kind of walking icon by the time I got to his university, a man
more known about than known. He'd taught for a very long
time, and his gestures and expressions grew more stylized and
exaggerated with every passing year. Like many others at
Virginia, I found myself as much taken with the way he looked

and spoke as with what he said. Scott had a way of scrunching up his face tightly and peering off into the imagined distance whenever he wanted to stop and contemplate an idea (which he would do, mid-sentence, for minutes at a time). He hardly ever looked at his students. If we had gotten up and left the room no doubt he would have continued to lecture grandiloquently.

His most pronounced expression was my favorite. It always came when he returned to emphasize that central tenet of the "New Criticism," the popular theory of reading he helped to articulate and promote. What, Scott would ask, in all our literary judgments, matters first and most? What matters first and only? He'd sit quietly before us, but brimming like a volcano, shaking his head a bit from side to side, staring at the ground, his mouth a perfect circle. Then, suddenly, dramatically, he would look up, eyes wide, hold aloft whatever book happened to be in his hand, and answer: "The *text!* The *text!*" The exclamation bounded off the cinder-block walls of our classroom.

It has stuck with me since. How can we approach the life and work of Jesus of Nazareth except by reading Matthew, Mark, Luke, or John? How but through the gospels can we know what he thinks, how he acts, what it is that he requires of his followers? Some will suggest church doctrine, or long-standing tradition, or even miraculous revelation of the Supreme Being. But doctrine and tradition derive from another kind of authority: Jesus claims that they're often based, not on "the commandments of God," but on "the precepts of men." As for divine revelation — that I patiently await. Yours, my friend, does me no good.

So what remains? "The *text!*" The Text, the Word, the Greatest Story Ever Told. That's what we have, the one thing Jews and Christians have always had. In the beginning was the Word, after all; everything else proceeds from that. The world grows out of it, and immediately starts to decay, but the Word continues, never changing, to the end. The Hebrews created a great Temple and a great Text. The Temple is gone, the Text remains.

The same can be said of the Temple called Jesus. "Heaven and earth will pass away," he claims, "but my words will not," and certainly the dogged endurance of the gospels in our mutable world is something of a marvel. Their continued presence is a source of comfort to Christians, but also of frustration, since they're the one obstacle to what we'd prefer to think about Jesus, the single impediment to every gospel according to us. Wherever we are in our lives, whatever we may want to claim about this Galilean, there they are, four stories of his life and work, always in front of us like a Hasid's phylactery, and built with that most basic and stubborn element of signification: word. So how are we to approach Jesus of Nazareth? "Continue in my word," he says — sound advice all around.

I had two other classes that first semester at Virginia, one on Shakespeare and the other on the New Testament. Texts aplenty! And in the Shakespeare seminar we wasted no time getting at them, working at close range, phrase by phrase, in play after play, savoring what was good, denouncing what was not, always with the words before us. Every class was interesting, propelled by the power of our engagement with the text. Only once did we lift our eyes from the page: when someone forwarded the theory that the Earl of Oxford wrote all of Shakespeare's plays. We spent more than an hour of good time chasing that idea around, searching for "clues" from the folios, fretting a little over the lack of historical evidence for the life of this man, born of humble circumstances, apparently unschooled, who grew to explore so powerfully the basic elements of the human soul. Finally, gratefully, we abandoned that snipe hunt and delved back into the great tome called the Riverside Shakespeare.

Maybe the Earl of Oxford wrote the New Testament too, because in my third class we never got to those texts. The gospels, in particular, we were careful to avoid, heading instead to the secondary sources. Why? Because, as the professor explained in our first meeting, they don't present us with the actual teachings of the historical Jesus. They are unable to offer us a reliable portrait of the man or his message. They depend on word of mouth, on hearsay, on stories that became more and more embellished with each re-telling. They reflect the concerns of the early Church — competition with Jewish authorities, the problem of the Gentiles, beliefs about the Second Coming, persecution from Rome — rather than the concerns of Jesus. The narratives are confused, contradictory, repetitive, out of chronological order. We can never really know Jesus by way of these ancient texts; he has been irretrievably lost.

Now clearly this was a breach of contract, a kind of high-brow mail fraud. I had bought a product featured in an attractive department brochure. And now the distributor claimed that it didn't exist.

Or was it a breach? Didn't I know perfectly well that this is what I would hear at Virginia, and at almost every institution of higher education in the country? I think I must have. In fact, it was probably even worse than that. At heart I felt the same about the gospels myself: if these were historical documents they were very strange ones indeed. So what were my grounds for complaint? What did I really want to hear in that class? What did I hope the gospels would be?

As a child of the Bible Belt I already knew the conservative position very well. I'd heard it again and again, on television and radio and from a great many schoolyard friends. They say that the gospels, and all of the Bible, are divinely inspired, and therefore "inerrant" in their reporting of what Jesus said and did. There is an unswerving literal sense to each sentence in the gospels by which these texts provide for us a specific and objective body of knowledge with a clear blueprint for action and thought that Christians should follow or lose that name. Analysis and discussion of the gospels do have their place. But in the end what we really need to do is treat each and every word as if it is carved in sacred stone.

This is an admirably unambiguous stance, commended by the power of its conviction. And yet I knew it wouldn't really get me any closer to the gospels, or their chosen subject, than I was already. In fact it left me in exactly the same place. Although the conservative approach is certainly different from the liberal one, it ends up producing the very same message about the gospels: Hands Off. The differing approaches then lead to a shared result. *Both cut off discussion of Jesus completely.* One says you can't touch; the other says you shouldn't.

Consider the debate over the gospels today. It's about eye-witness accounts and the work of later editors, apparent inconsistencies between the four narratives and the power of divine inspiration, concerns of the early Church and extra-canonical corroboration and the latest spade-work in the desert. It isn't about Jesus at all. Almost as if they are afraid of what will happen if they have to deal with Jesus' teachings as they are presented in the gospels, students, church people, and scholars tend to avoid actually getting their hands on them. Say the conservatives: just accept the literal words and leave them alone. End of discussion. Reply the liberals: forget trying to discover the authentic Jesus in the gospels. Case closed. A kind of kitchen industry has sprung up over this debate, and the professionals on both sides are warmed nicely by the heat they generate. (I am ignoring for the purpose of argument many good works of faith and scholarship that fall in with neither camp.) The two extremes stand in an opposition that is also a kind of symbiosis. And the effect of this symbiosis is the one you might least expect — the muting of meaningful discussion about the teachings of Jesus of Nazareth as they are presented in the four gospels.

Not even the Pharisees and disciples were this difficult. Imagine Jesus telling a story about a father and his wayward son. A small group of people gathers before him, lawyers and priests and common folk alike, and all are listening carefully. The story is told, and shortly ends. The group then sits quietly for a moment to take it in, to ponder its implications. What can such a thing mean? What does it say about the possibilities and consequences of forgiveness within our relationships? All sit in thoughtful silence. Then, suddenly, a Pharisee steps up and says, "That's not historically accurate. There was no such family as the one you speak of." A disciple stands and shouts back "Yes there was! Jesus, this great teacher, inspired by God, said so. It must be literally true." The two argue back and forth for a while, loud and strident, each moved by his own earnestness, thankful that he is a man of conviction and no prodigal. Somehow they "strain a gnat and swallow a camel," to use Jesus' phrase. And in the meantime that parable, the brilliant tale of the wayward son, goes unconsidered. Jesus suggests that our clever diversions allow us to avoid considering what has been said, and thereby manage to ignore the demands that it makes on our lives. He quotes the bitter protest of his favorite prophet, Isaiah:

> *You will indeed listen, but never understand, and you will indeed look, but never perceive. For this people's heart has grown dull, and their ears are heavy of hearing, and they have shut their eyes; so that they might not look with their eyes, and listen with their ears, and understand with their heart.*

◆   ◆   ◆

The quest for "the historical Jesus" is a peculiar one. In almost every book written on the subject — and there are half a dozen new ones every year — the author begins by saying that it's impossible to know exactly what Jesus really said and did. Then, unaccountably, he or she sets off in pursuit of that knowledge. Maybe the joy is in the pursuit and not the capture, although if that's the case we might just as happily pursue a heffalump. But these scholars should heed their own warnings. If our goal is the capture of the historical Jesus then we've failed before we begin. If the only tool we have to approach him is textual and historical reconstruction, theology as archaeology, then we're going to have to console ourselves by playing with a few ancient and broken building blocks scattered on the ground where once we think a Temple stood.

It's true, of course. In our search for "the facts" about Jesus of Nazareth the gospels do fail us. But they fail on our terms, not on theirs. Matthew isn't interested in writing a history, like Josephus' *Jewish Antiquities*. Mark doesn't want just to compile a collection of sayings, like those of Confucius. John doesn't slowly build a logical argument, as in Plato's *Crito*. None of the existing categories applies. The form of composition called "gospel" has no exact parallel; it's unique to world literature. The only term I know of to describe it is Luke's: *narrative*, the recounting of a tale. Gospel is a kind of story.

It isn't by chance that all four of those texts concerning Jesus of Nazareth take a narrative format. (How odd we take for granted that they do!) Why don't the gospel writers choose a Socratic dialogue, or a history, or an anthology of aphorisms, or a mystical reverie instead? The answer, of course, lies in their chosen subject. Here, as in all great literature, form mirrors content. Each gospel story takes as its subject a teller of stories, a man who "would speak... only in parables," who speaks even of *himself* in the third person. Jesus apparently thinks that *story* best explains who he is and what he hopes to achieve (as he believes it does for everyone). History stays in the past, and therefore lacks the urgency and immediacy of experience that Jesus is seeking. Philosophy is abstract, and reason finally unconvincing. The Pharisees' method of structured argument, law, and proof may appeal to the head, but does not satisfy the heart. What's left? Story. Stories are immediate, immanent, piquant, urgent, and ongoing — just as life is. All lived experience has a narrative nature. Jesus knows that nothing can rival a story's engagement with its reader or listener. Philosophy and history are matters of the head. Only by way of story can people "understand with their heart." So Jesus is a teller of stories — traditional stories about Jonah, Elijah, Elisha, Moses, Noah, Solomon, David, and parables of his own devising. To make his message immediate and urgent he narrates it, puts it in time and space, and gives it a human dimension. A steward is so greedy he grabs his neighbor by the throat to get a few pennies he's owed. A woman is so desperate and determined she unceasingly appeals to a judge she knows is unjust. A man is so hungry he eats the food he feeds to pigs.

Consider the techniques of the storyteller and rural poet: irony and understatement, contradiction and hyperbole, paradox, personification, and pun. Humor is a particular strength. He nicknames the loudmouthed James and John "Sons of Thunder." He discovers the likeness of the owner of a coin on the coin itself. When approached by a crowd threatening bodily harm Jesus plays it hilariously deadpan: "Doubtless you will quote me the proverb 'Physician, heal thyself'." Some of his best humor comes by way of understatement and overstatement. Once he tells the disciples to sell their mantles to buy swords. Anxious for armed insurrection against Rome, they reply excitedly that they have two already. Good, says Jesus, that's enough. He speaks of camels being swallowed or passing through eyes of needles; he pictures great mountains cast into the sea. He pushes his metaphors to the limits of signification, employing a feminine image for himself (a mother hen brooding over her chicks), calling God "Papa" (Abba), comparing heaven to a mustard seed. He loves irony — the meek inheriting the earth, the prophets dying in Jerusalem, things hidden from the wise and revealed to children. He lives by paradox — you must die to live, give to get, be last to be first. And contradiction — he says he is sent only to the House of Israel but plans to "make disciples of all nations," calls down judgment upon the world but insists he came only to save it, says there will be no signs for the coming of the kingdom and lists a few. (I'm reminded of Walt Whitman, America's Blake: "Do I contradict myself? Very well, I contradict myself. I contain *multitudes.*")

Jesus also makes of his own life a good story, one that he dramatizes in many clever ways. His acts are small tales within the tale, a series of performed parables to complement the narrated ones. The characters are the same: rich and poor, vengeful and merciful, the working and idle, Gentile and Jew. The setting is the fields and roads and homes of Judea. After a while it gets hard to remember which is an event and which a story. Cursing a fig tree, washing a poor man's feet, throwing money-changers out of the Temple — these productions are not of much practical or historical value. Surely the money changers are back the very next day. These are above all enacted stories, reality theater, stark epiphanies that begin in the realm of experience and point outward from it.

Even the way Jesus tells a tale can be a kind of enacted parable in itself, of one piece with the moment and its setting. Imagine a tired day-laborer, ploughing in the hot sun. At the edge of his fields he sees a young rabbi preparing to speak to an assembled group. He draws near; the rabbi begins. "A sower sowed his seed on the ground. Some fell on rocky ground and was eaten by birds. Some fell on weedy ground and was choked. Some fell on shallow soil, sprouted, and shriveled. But some fell on good soil and grew. Good afternoon." And the rabbi moves on. Now what will the laborer think of this? Is it a sermon? Is it a riddle? A lecture on agronomy, given by a rabbi to a farmer? Hard to say. It was quite a scene, though, and he has the rest of his long day to turn it over in his head.

Jesus provides yet another service within the gospels. Not only is he the teller. Not only is he the tale. He even supplies the hermeneutic instruction for approaching and understanding it. "Take care how you listen," he counsels his followers, and offers specific advice on how to listen to story, how to think about symbol. This is an area of great interest to Jesus, a gifted exegete and one of the first critical theorists, though he's not mentioned in any surveys of critical theory.

Most significantly, Jesus is the first to question whether the tools of reason are sufficient to approaching a story, an image, or a person, or whether some other mode of apprehension is required. In other words, he doesn't just question various modes of critical engagement with the world — he questions _the idea of criticism itself_ by suggesting that true revelation comes only through faith. "Become as a little child," he famously advises his disciples. Why? Maybe because children have an abundance of deep feeling and imagination, the primary tools of faith, and thereby can engage a story or person or event in ways adults can't or won't. Jesus argues that only _faith_ can allow people to understand him, because he speaks in story and symbol, and because much of what he says is so offensive that only faith can digest it. This is for him the interpretive key, the reason his lessons are often "hidden from the learned and wise and revealed to children." (They are certainly hidden from the disciples and Pharisees. Like most conservatives, the disciples lack the imagination needed to approach Jesus' stories profitably; like most liberals, the Pharisees lack the faith.)

The great Bible stories resonate more deeply in children than in adults, partly because their imagination allows them to enter into stories unconditionally. Children don't have to suspend disbelief to appreciate a story. They never suspended their _belief!_ They don't require that a story provide some external justification for itself, historical or otherwise. Good stories are their own reason for being. Children allow stories to work their peculiar magic, to take them and transform them, let them see, hear, and feel remarkable new things by means of the redemptive power of the imagination. "Why is the Bible more Entertaining & Instructive than any other book?" Blake asks of a minister who dislikes the imaginative exercise of his engravings. "Is it not because [it is] addressed to the Imagination, which is Spiritual Sensation, and but mediately to the Understanding or Reason?"

The gospels are stories. And like all good stories they stretch our credulity. They describe events well outside the limits of our experience and actually expect us to believe them. That stretch is the warm-up for the leap of faith it anticipates. The gospels refuse us objective knowledge about their subject because the subject himself teaches a way of faith rather than of knowledge — Isaiah's "understanding of the heart." Knowledge can take us to a certain point in our spiritual development. But it passes away. We will never be able to build a bridge over a chasm that can be crossed only with a leap of faith. Maybe those who aren't concerned with compiling empirical evidence for Jesus' life and work, those who "have never seen," really are "more blessed" than those who have. They don't wait for the promised bridge; they've leapt already.

◆   ◆   ◆

Here is the paradox at the source of our misreadings. Infinite truth is spiritual rather than material. But Jesus believes that the best way to illustrate any kind of truth in a material world is by way of material objects and events. Of course, material beings, fresh from the clay, naturally have a hard time understanding that those objects themselves are never the source of value and truth, but can stand only as figures for what completely transcends them. In fact, devotion to those specific objects and events may serve to obscure the great truth of what they're designed to reveal. Jesus points this out to the disciple Thomas: truth goes far beyond the holes in a man's hands and feet. He argues that truth is always a matter of Spirit. But how can you build a bridge out of Spirit? Jesus says that "those who are of the spirit are like the wind." But how can you document a life like the wind?

We can't. It eludes us. Jesus remains outside our historical records, and his chosen symbols won't fit in our reliquaries. And yet our work to obtain and appropriate him goes on, year after year. Often our project in reading the gospels is to reduce Jesus' life and words to certain specific "facts" — chunks of historical or literal knowledge that can be stacked in a pile, stamped "AUTHENTIC" or "USEFUL," and then set to our purposes. We act like the Pharisees, whom Jesus says "pore over the scriptures, believing that in them [they] can find eternal life." We mine the gospels like quarries from which we cut blocks to construct towers to heaven. Or we reduce them to Pythagorean formulas, one of which we hope will be the password to eternity (tenure, too, is forever). Jesus' expression "born again" has been used in just this way, an astonishing image that in some Christian circles has been reduced to little more than "Open Sesame."

The solution to our misunderstandings may lie in finding images powerful and evocative enough to spark the dull minds of hide-bound creatures, but too far "out there" to be made into idols of their own. In the gospels we often see Jesus trying to do just that, mulling over his choice of available objects, deciding how to illustrate the infinite in a finite context, struggling to find a startling simile for something that is only itself and nothing else. "What is the kingdom of heaven like?" he muses out loud. "What shall I compare it with?" And he always comes up with something, an object unexpected, sometimes offensive, and often more than a little stretched. The effort required to follow the comparison is very great — Jesus shouldn't be so surprised that few manage it. But maybe he intends it only as an imaginative exercise anyway, a kind of spiritual calisthenics, designed to roust people out of the lethargy of their thinking and feeling. The kingdom of heaven is like... a mustard seed? From which grows a wild and scraggly shrub? A fish net? Notoriously smelly and unreliable? *Yeast?* When only unleavened bread is holy?

It's hard to see how, when faced with these fertile fields, our approaches to the gospels can present us with such a meager harvest. The gospels' conception of Jesus — Word as Flesh — seems so much fuller than our own, where his words are treated like great stone idols. I heard a sermon a few years back in which the minister, preaching on a carefully sectioned piece of gospel, argued that Jesus clearly condemns people to the darkness and death of Gehenna. There men will weep and gnash their teeth. Jesus said it, plain and clear, and yet some say that everyone is going to be saved, that no one is going to hell for what they do in this life. These people don't take Jesus "at his word," as the minister put it. The choice for Christians is obvious: we need to take what Jesus said and believe it.

This is a strong and faith-filled approach to a text that can bear the weight of such devotion. The only question is whether the heart of "his word" is its particular expressions and images, or the infinite truth toward which it points. Jesus does talk about a hellish pit called Gehenna. He also says that if your right eye leads you to sin, you should pluck it out of its socket and cast it away. Ridiculous as it sounds, this is a course of action Jesus recommends. Would the minister read him "at his word" here? Well, we all pick and choose (from Jesus and everyone) what we need to live, though you can be sure that somewhere, some time, somebody ripped an eye out in an attempt to save his immortal soul. The human mind is too taken with the material world to imagine anything beyond it. Remember Jesus' late-night discussion with the Pharisee Nicodemus. Jesus tells him that he "must be born again." Nicodemus thinks about this for a minute. And then the grandfather of all literalists asks his inevitable question: "Lord, how can a man crawl back in his mother's womb?" This may be the greatest comedic moment in the gospels. Of course, the literal-minded can't see gospel as comedy; here the joke is at their expense.

Jesus describes the horror and misery of all poor souls who are not prepared for the arrival of the bridegroom. He also speaks of a shepherd not content with his ninety-nine sheep, who searches tirelessly until he brings that one lost sheep home, rejoicing all the way. Now one parable may hint at the soul's damnation, and another at its salvation. But remember that Jesus is talking about *shepherds* and *bridegrooms*, though he never literally tends sheep, and never literally marries. Try as we may, we can't shoehorn these images into our custom-made doctrines and traditions. "Gehenna," you ask? It was a refuse dump south of Jerusalem.

It's not easy to talk objectively about images of bridegrooms and landfills. When a man says that he's like someone about to be married — what does that mean? Oh, there are hundreds of possibilities. The image provokes in the mind all sorts of interesting and provocative ideas, and maybe that's what Jesus intends with it. And yet none is inevitably *the one*, a thing, a cold fact you can lay your hands on and turn to your purposes. The image opens up possibilities, but it doesn't necessarily help narrow them down again. Is it that Jesus is anxiously awaiting a great event? Must be. Is it that he'll choose to whom or what he will unite himself? Hmm. Will he take more brides than one? Maybe. (Is that allowed?) Will his choice be a celebration? Who are these bridesmaids, and what is their role in all of this? Do they have anything other to do than wait with well-trimmed lamps? What? *Lamps?*

None of us can say with certainty what all of this means. The images offer so much and guarantee nothing. You can't speak definitively about such things, or use them to pin Jesus down once and for all. And this is the true source of scholarship's frustration with the gospels. Like his contemporaries, we may finally lose patience with his methods. "How long will you keep us in suspense?" a group of followers complains on one occasion. "If you are the Christ tell us *plainly*." And Jesus starts up again about sheep and shepherds.

Consider "Son of Man," Jesus' single most favorite phrase, the one with which he seems, obliquely and tantalizingly, to refer to himself. You can't get around the title — Jesus uses it eighty times in four gospels (and a peculiar moniker it is for someone who says he "and the Father are one"). "Son of Man" is a common idiomatic expression that usually means "human being." Every human being is a son or daughter of "man" (in Hebrew, "Adam"). But it also suggests something else, something very different. In mystical literature of Jesus' time it's the title of an apocalyptic figure of great power: "I saw visions in the night, and behold, with the clouds of heaven, there came one like a son of man." This Son of Man is a mystical being, a harbinger of salvation or retribution, a maker of epochs. You might think it ridiculous to harness a meaning so mystical to one so mundane, yet "Son of Man" does that, and surely it's that paradox, the absurd juxtaposition of finite and infinite, that Jesus finds appealing. Still, nothing concrete can be made of the title.

The same is true of the title "Son of God." C. S. Lewis has famously argued that Jesus of Nazareth must be either "Son of God" or "devil of hell." If he does not properly own the first title then he's a charlatan, unworthy of our faith and devotion. This is probably true, but what Lewis expects us to make of it is unclear. To see Jesus as Son of God is the *beginning* of our understanding, not the end of it. The title "Son of God" is not like the title "Queen of England." There are no well-defined attributes, duties, and obligations. (By contrast, "devil of hell" seems downright plain.) You can't talk with easy authority about what it is to be the Son of God, and those who most often use the term never even try. Words crumble beneath the weight of the mystery.

The sayings and stories and expressions and character and actions of Jesus can't be condensed into *things*. This is what most biblical scholarship has attempted and failed to do over the last century, and managed somehow to be proud of its failure. It may or may not be true that the "historical" Jesus has been lost. But before we exhaust all our energies rolling this thing up the hill again we should pause and ask one question: is Jesus himself interested in being known as an historical figure? Well, he is certainly leery of "what... people say about me," and probably should be. He's forever being labeled by his contemporaries as one thing or another, from demon to Elijah. Of course, all historical categories are distortions; Jesus himself avoids them. And yet that hasn't dissuaded us from trying to capture him thus, and thinking we almost have him, and failing, and trying again. Like the disciples, we rejoice to have him in our home, but wake the next morning to find that he's already moved on. Like his female followers, we go to attend him in the tomb, but find that it doesn't contain him either. Like the witnesses at his trial, we compile our evidence about him, and present it in forum, but our findings conflict, and finally prove nothing. Histories and semantics, like temples, trials, and tombs, all fail to capture the man.

Jesus himself chooses other means of expressing his person: a conversation, an ablution, a meal. And, above all, a story. In the gospels we have four texts woven around one subject (Latin *textum* — "a thing woven"), none particularly long or short, written at different times, by different authors and, like all stories, filled with differing impressions and remembrances and feelings about who they met and what they saw and heard. But that doesn't mean these texts fail in presenting Jesus of Nazareth to us. Like their protagonist, the gospel writers understand the narrative nature of lived experience. They present Jesus to us the way we experience *all* people — through anecdote and gossip (a word closely related to "gospel"), impression and image, feeling and remembrance — a subjective and perfectly human way to meet this Jew, who is always a subject and never an object, and who engages life on a personal level rather than an historical one.

In the long run it may be a great blessing that we'll never find Historical Jesus, the Holy Grail of biblical scholarship. Our failure may finally prompt us to forsake this idol and return to the Word. In fact many biblical scholars today *are* starting to rediscover the gospels as stories, and doing with them what children have always done. That can't help but be a deeper and more fruitful engagement than the ones offered to us by modern liberal and conservative scholarship, by the Pharisees and disciples of our own fractured age. The four gospels offer us so much more — the chance to hear an unusual man, to watch him face his various triumphs and failures, to feel something of what he feels, to contemplate his unique vision of the world, and to witness his exercises in the discipline of love and self-sacrifice.

PART II

III

PETRIFIED

The Roman Virtues, Warlike Fame
Take Jesus' and Jehovah's Name

"The Everlasting Gospel"

IT'S A PECULIAR situation. Jesus is the most famous figure in human history and the most misunderstood, a legend and a cipher, a man worshipped and unknown. But maybe this is to be expected. After all, two thousand years separate us from him. Add to this the obstacles of distance, culture, and language, and our failures begin to look less woeful. Aren't those the real source of our problems, the true cause of our misapprehensions, more than what he says and the way he says it? No. Read the gospels and you'll find it every bit as true of the first century as of the twentieth: the people who love Jesus, and the ones who hate him, all do so without a clear idea of who he is or what he's talking about.

Consider for example his disciples, the special twelve, hand-picked by Jesus to join him in his life and work. These chosen few follow him throughout the lands of Palestine, hear his message preached, and witness his ministry from its beginning to its abrupt end. You would think that if any have ever understood Jesus, been challenged and transformed by his parables, got beyond the offense of his teachings simply to believe, it would have to be these. And, through the ages, the disciples have indeed been touted as our models, exemplars of the faith, trustees of the gospel message, men of action and insight whom we would do well to emulate.

So you might be surprised to find in the gospels, as I was when I first began to read them, that the disciples are an astoundingly ignorant, selfish, and faithless lot. Jesus sums them up well: "foolish men, and slow of heart." They bicker over their relative greatness. They react blankly to Jesus' parables, and upbraid him for teaching in that manner. They second-guess his decisions. They obstruct women and children who want to speak with him. They fail him completely in the last moments of his life. His favorite three fall asleep when he needs them most, his own treasurer sells him to the authorities, and the rest scatter to protect their lives.

How is it, then, that we still tend to like and admire the disciples? It's because, in spite of their many transgressions, the gospels still manage to paint them as sympathetic figures — a feat of uncanny narrative skill. When the twelve act in a bumbling or faithless manner they come across as simple country people, and forgivably quaint; there's something endearing in their constant, wide-eyed wonder. Their ignorance often looks more like naiveté, and their selfish squabbling like sibling rivalry. All in all the disciples appear as a rather ordinary group of young men — inquisitive and obtuse, courageous and cowardly, loyal and self-centered — who become fascinated with the man Jesus. Perhaps they're likable as much because of as in spite of their many faults. At the very least you can't help but be moved by their quixotic devotion to a movement whose purpose, by their own admission, is largely unknown to them.

Their head and emblem is Peter, whom the church has dubbed "Prince of the Apostles." There are no fewer than nine Simons in the New Testament, but Jesus' renaming of the first one begins to set him apart, and Simon Peter does the rest. In him the gospels present us with one of the most unforgettable figures in all of literature. He is big, boisterous, foolish but painfully well-intentioned, and almost perfectly transparent, a man who speaks and acts without deception or diplomacy. Peter is one of those rare people who can't act like anything other than what they are. His every thought is acted upon; every emotion is written plainly on his brow. Whatever is intended is instantly attempted. Whatever is on his mind is also on his tongue. And so a great array of basic human faults and strengths appears on display in the person of Simon Peter, writ large upon this large man.

It is Peter's simple humanness, above all else, that constitutes his most salient feature. What makes him important to the gospel narratives is not that he's special, but that he's typical, a model of the human mind at work. Peter has many faults, and all are instructive ones. When he and Jesus stand side by side, as they so often do, even the poorest reader can see the difference between them. (As Blake says, though with more than a touch of irony, "If others had not been foolish, we should be so.") And yet, in spite of them all, including the most heinous sin of betrayal, Peter remains a likable character. His Everyman fallibility makes him an oddly comforting presence in the gospels. The cold and self-contained Judas is clearly more intelligent and competent than Peter, but that doesn't improve our opinion of him. Both betray Jesus, but Judas seems monstrous to us, and Peter is now a saint.

Peter and Jesus first meet in Capernaum. Both are recent arrivals, one from Bethsaida and the other from Nazareth. Peter and his brother Andrew are partners with James and John in a fishing enterprise on the Lake of Gennesaret, and it is there Jesus calls on him. Jesus heals his mother-in-law of a fever when he visits his house, and from then on the two are almost never apart. Peter quickly assumes the role of mouthpiece for all the disciples — asking questions, cajoling Jesus to explain his behavior, unpack a parable, share his travel plans, hint at what he hopes to accomplish. Sometimes he expresses just the right note of wonder. At others he blurts out exactly the wrong thing. But in every case Peter plays a crucial role in the narrative. He is the garrulous sidekick, just the loud and obstinate interlocutor

Socrates needed but never found, someone who can provoke interesting responses from his teacher time and again. Many of the gospels' central thematic motifs grow out of their conflicts and discussions.

The relationship between Jesus and Peter is the central one of the gospels, but it's complex and problematic. Jesus obviously feels a real fondness for his first lieutenant, and requires his company on crucial occasions. Yet he constantly expresses doubts about his reliability. He warns Peter that Satan has "demanded to have you, that he might sift you like wheat." (Another great image — it is too often, and with the ease of sifting, that Peter is "had.") Throughout his ministry Jesus alternates praise and chastisement for Peter, and he does little to resolve the paradox of his commitment to the man. With practically the same breath he rebukes him for his lack of faith and praises him for ideas that transcend "flesh and blood." He promises Peter a special role in establishing "the kingdom" and calls him no less than "Satan." He dubs him "Rock" — a clever pun that works both in Greek and Aramaic. But his metaphoric meaning is itself two-pronged, and marvelously insinuated, hinted at now and again, referring arcanely to the bane and boon that is Peter. In one of his best-known parables Jesus speaks of a farmer who sowed his seed broadly upon the ground. The seed that fell on rock only withered and died. In another he tells of two houses, one foolishly built upon sand, which fell when rains and wind tested it. The house built upon the solid foundation of rock endured. On one occasion Jesus tells Peter that he is just such a sure foundation. On another he calls him a "stumbling block" — a troublesome rock obstruction.

Of course, "Rock" is also a universal nickname for someone reputed to lack intelligence, and this may be the first thing you notice about Peter. He knows fishing; everything else has to be explained. Like the other disciples, throughout his life Peter has used his hands a great deal and his head rather less. As a result he sometimes lacks the intelligence and imagination needed to approach Jesus' words and stories profitably. When Jesus preaches the coming of a new kingdom Peter wants to gather up all the available swords. When he tells the disciples to forgive others Peter wants to know exactly how many times. As many as seven, he asks? (Jesus teases him. An exact number? 490.) When Peter sees a vision of a transformed Jesus standing in shimmering robes beside Moses and Elijah he suggests that they put up three shelters ("not knowing what he said," the narrator humorously explains). This is all his mind can supply him with, stuck as it is in the world of *things*. If the visions had remained no doubt Simple Simon would have offered to make a run for bread and fish. This is what's important to him. He's soon lost when Jesus speaks of a reality that transcends whole bread and wood shacks.

Even after on-the-spot exegesis from the man they call "Master" Peter and the other disciples are baffled by Jesus' stories and images. In fact they often complain about them, demanding that Jesus speak "plainly," as if he's just being pointlessly obtuse. But they themselves are the obtuse ones, demonstrating time and again that they're capable of thinking only in the most conventional and material terms. Jesus hoped to teach by way of symbolic acts, like the feeding of thousands at the seaside, but no such luck. The disciples are too busy "gathering up broken pieces of bread and fish" to consider what such a thing could possibly mean, and Jesus impatiently commands them to return to their boat. They scurry back, forgetting to take any of the remaining bread with them. There he tries to explain again, but without success: "they had not understood what the miracle meant; their minds were closed." The twelve can't conceive of an existence that isn't centered on the getting and eating of bread, so the bread is all they care about. When Jesus goes on to warn them of the corrupting "yeast of the Pharisees and of Herod" they protest that they have no bread, still thinking ruefully of those baskets left on the shore. Jesus is incredulous: "How could you fail to understand that I was not talking about bread?"

Even when Jesus offers a specific interpretation of a parable to the twelve it doesn't do much good. Their confusion is palpable. (Imagine Peter's bewildered reply: "The farmer's sowing *word*?") Jesus eventually becomes exasperated by such thickheadedness. "How much longer must I put up with you?" he fumes. This frustration proves counterproductive; later when he tells a story or performs a symbolic act the disciples are "afraid to ask him what it meant."

♦   ♦   ♦

Peter provides much of the physical as well as ideological drama in the gospels. The man is unused to forethought or reflection; he acts mostly on impulse and gut feeling, and this leads to some interesting situations. (We meet a far more circumspect Peter, for better and worse, in the book of Acts.) When he sees Jesus walking on water Peter tries to master the feat himself, and promptly begins to sink (like a Rock). When Jesus is seized in the Garden of Gethsemane Peter lifts his sword and lops off the right ear of the high priest's slave. When he's suddenly confronted with having to betray either himself or Jesus he instinctively lies to save his life, even though a few hours earlier he had earnestly sworn never to deny his "Lord." Now these kinds of behaviors appear to be random or impulsive, but they also reveal a key element of his character: Peter is self-serving. His actions are designed to bring him a kind of glory, or to preserve his life or reputation. To walk on water, to fight when hopelessly outnumbered, to swear loudly that, although others may become offended and fall away, you never will — these are grandiose performances whose focus is always Peter.

From the day he first joins Jesus Peter keeps himself in the fore. In exchange for abandoning his fishing business he expects a certain payback; this latest enterprise is not one he undertakes altruistically. "We have left everything and followed you," he reminds Jesus. "What therefore shall we have?" (This same attitude is later displayed by other disciples as well. James and John are most brazen: "Teacher, we want you to do for us whatever we ask of you.") We witness Peter's habits of self-solicitude not only during Jesus' ministry but throughout his life, even during his usually powerful and triumphant evangelizing missions. Consider the incident that takes place when he travels to Antioch, where he and his wife stay and work and eat with Gentile believers. Things go well there until other Jewish Christians arrive. Then Peter begins to worry that reports about his eating with Gentiles will damage his reputation with the folks back in Jerusalem (whom Paul calls "the circumcision faction"). So he abandons the locals entirely. The consequences are devastating for the infant community at Antioch. Peter is certainly here the stumbling block, the obstructing Rock, Jesus called him many years earlier. His "insincerity" spreads among the Jews there, according to Paul, corrupting even Barnabas. Paul finally "opposed him to his face," reminding him that "we are not reckoned righteous by works of the law, but through faith." There is no word on Peter's response. Maybe he repented under the full weight of Paul's rebuke. But his flip-flop on this issue is a particularly galling one: it was Peter himself who had once asked Jesus to explain why his followers are not bound by Jewish food regulations.

Of course, this is only one side of the story. Peter is also capable of great selflessness, altruism, and personal sacrifice. His devotion to the movement, and to Jesus in particular, is fierce and visceral. It's easy to picture Peter, large and earnest, a hulking presence in any room, despondent that his Master might suffer any pain or indignity. He would gladly suffer for him. "Lord, I would be ready to go to prison with you, and to death," he exclaims. Until the arrest Peter is willing to risk everything, even his life, to promote Jesus' ministry, to preserve him from the hand of his enemies, to help overthrow the much-despised Roman governor and establish the kingdom of heaven upon earth. Consider again that reckless attack on Malchus, a slave in the contingent sent to arrest Jesus in Gethsemane. There Peter shows complete disregard for his own well-being in defense of his beloved leader. And yet that same night, to save the very life he risked a few hours earlier, he curses, even swears an oath before various witnesses that he "never knew" Jesus (an ironic confession if ever there was one).

This looks at first like a very dramatic change of heart, but closer reading suggests other motivations at work. The act is willful rather than brave: notice that he strikes, not one of the soldiers, but an unarmed slave. And his brandishing the sword couldn't be much help to Jesus anyway, since Peter stands alone against a number of well-armed Romans. It works only as theater, a final gesture made to convince Jesus that he really does love him but has a hard time staying awake on a bellyful of Passover wine. The act is all about Peter, and nothing about Jesus, so his complete about-face isn't really that surprising. Within those few decisive hours Jesus had been thrown in prison; for Peter the great drama had come to its end. He certainly had high hopes for this charismatic movement, and for the man he believed could never die. Those hopes die hard in hard times.

Until Jesus' arrest Peter and the other disciples quietly cherish a belief that they have found their savior with a sword, one who will establish a glorious Jewish empire and trample the mighty legions of Rome and the occupying government they hate completely. Their desperate dependence on this hope is certainly understandable. The Romans tax their meager earnings. They hassle their family and friends. They restrict their trade, subjugate their kings, mock their religion. The disciples know the prophecies about a Messiah who would "shatter the unrighteous rulers, break them to pieces with a rod of iron," and their fondest hopes are set on that day. One disciple, another Simon, is a Zealot. Judas' name, Iscariot, identifies him as a member of the dagger-carrying Sicarii, the clandestine terrorist group. These men wait to exact their revenge on the Romans at the first opportunity. Peter even carries a sword during the Passover.

The twelve are not alone in this hope. It's what most Jews pray for — another King David, perhaps, to slay this latest Goliath. Those in the throng that shout "Hosanna!" (*"Save Us!"*) to Jesus during his triumphal entry into Jerusalem probably expect him to start an armed insurrection against the forces of the Empire, as many had before, and even more would in decades to come. "Blessed is the coming kingdom of our ancestor David!" they roar. His popularity in the Holy City plummets overnight when they realize Jesus won't accommodate them in this, and from that point on his execution is all but inevitable. The Jews naturally prefer a common bandit like Barabbas to such a man. Their disappointment in him is palpable, summed up in glum remarks made by two unnamed followers after his death: "Our hopes had been that he would be the one to set Israel free."

Of course, they should all have seen this long before his final entry into Jerusalem. Jesus never expresses the slightest interest in establishing a political kingdom. "My kingdom is not from this world," he tells a sympathetic Pilate. "If it were my followers would fight." He couldn't be much "plainer" than that. Although the crowds demand insurrection, Jesus always preaches resurrection. His clearly avowed intention is to take a message of nationalist hope and fashion from it a vision of universal salvation.

Why this approach? Maybe Jesus believes that nationalism is just one more expression of basic human selfishness. Perhaps he feels that his countrymen need to be saved from themselves more than they need to be saved from others. It's hard to say, because there's little here to work with — Jesus avoids commenting on most of the prominent national issues of his day. But apparently he doesn't see the Romans as a problem in the first place. (In fact, he recommends that his followers perform specific acts of kindness for the occupying soldiers, and he himself heals a centurion's boy.) After pagan Rome there would be many other powers and principalities, as there had been many before them, and each rises and passes away in succession. What's the point of opposing something that will die on its own? (The next empire, by the way, was the Holy Roman. *Holy Roman.* Is any grave more restless than Peter's?)

Jesus' whole idea of "power," and his strategy for claiming it, is dramatically different from that of the disciples. His is the paradoxical method of *relinquishing* that power. Rather than aspire to lord it over these people, Jesus says he wants to serve them. "The Son of Man came not to be served but to serve," he insists, and instructs the others to follow in his example. "The greatest among you should be like the youngest," he tells the disciples, "and the one who rules like the one who serves." He takes James and John aside when they demand greater power within the movement and makes it clear that the New Creation must not be filled in with all the familiar furniture of the old: "You know that among the Gentiles those they call their rulers lord it over them, and their great men make their authority felt. Among you this is not to happen."

Jesus himself is the model for this new kind of authority, one that expresses itself in powerlessness, and Peter is its most vocal critic. Throughout the gospels the two men engage in a running debate over the nature and uses of power. When Peter calls Jesus "the Chosen One of God" he's praised for holding a faith that transcends finite understanding. But when Jesus tells him what it means to be chosen of God — suffering and death — Peter loudly admonishes him, and Jesus again points to the single cause of all their disagreements: "You are thinking not as God thinks but as human beings do." After that pivotal exchange Jesus begins to build on this, his strangest of teachings, expressing it in ever more trenchant and astonishing ways. Consider the scene in which he performs the ministering act of the lowliest servant, washing his disciples' feet before their final meal. This is almost more than Peter can bear. He can't imagine his Master as servant of all, and tells him as much. Later that same night it all comes to a head; Peter actually reaches for a sword to stop Jesus from undertaking his final act of submission. But now there's nothing more to be done, and Jesus' last words to Peter before his death are spoken more to himself: "Am I not to drink the cup that the Father has given me?"

♦   ♦   ♦

Jesus often calls the disciples "you of little faith." Their chronic faithlessness isn't expressed in the fact that Peter can't walk on water — Jesus never asked him to. The problem is that he thinks he *has to* in order to succeed, that miraculous displays of power are the whole reason for having a faith in the first place.

The disciples treat the power of faith as a magical tool that will let them control whomever and whatever they please, a spiritual contraption that can be set to their purposes, to lead them to building, bread, and sword, the only symbols of power they can imagine. They have never seen power that doesn't come from behind a sword, and are fooled by Jesus' facetious command to buy some. They have never known a peasant life that doesn't revolve around the getting and eating of bread, and think that bread alone is enough to live by. They have never heard of a deity that isn't housed in a building, and are easily impressed by the works of human hands (as upon their entrance to Jerusalem: "Look, Teacher! What massive stones! What magnificent buildings!"). This misapprehension is the source of their quandary. The disciples can't imagine that they need not rely on building, bread, and sword. They've forgotten that those are the tools of the Adversary, the very items offered to Jesus in the wilderness.

The twelve do enjoy many marvelous successes in their ministries. But of course they can't always *make* their fellow men and women behave in the ways they want. And if they can't, their faith begins to waver and wane. Whenever they get stuck, caught without resources, failing to heal one man or to convert another, and end up on the run, dodging civil authorities and menacing crowds, they are honestly dumbfounded. Why did the Spirit fail them? They certainly never blame themselves; the fault always lies elsewhere. So James and John ask Jesus to call down "fire from heaven" to scourge rude and unreceptive villagers. This is what they expect: a god who will prove his power at their behest. Jesus continues to insist that "the Son of Man came not to destroy the world but to save it," and says he'll give "no sign to this evil generation" but the sign of "Jonah" and "the Queen of the South." It's not clear what *that* means. But it is clear that the disciples' reliance on supernatural power for control and reassurance is misplaced. For Jesus, faith is the gift of those who don't require "proof." It can be adopted only by free choice, not compelled by otherworldly displays. So he contends that those who "haven't seen" are actually more blessed!

The disciples steadfastly refuse to accept Jesus' stance on this issue. For them divine intervention is the coin and commerce of faith. Jesus tries without success to redirect their focus. "Do not rejoice that the spirits submit to you," he says on one occasion. "Rejoice that your names are written in heaven." But the twelve continue to rely largely on signs and wonders for direction and encouragement, misunderstanding the nature of faith as badly as they misunderstand the gentle Spirit that is its manifestation. When they get together to replace Judas in the group of twelve, how do they decide? Not by prayer and careful consideration. They cast dice, like a pack of Roman soldiers, servants of a god that fits in their pockets. Of course Jesus had never done or taught any such thing. But Jesus is nowhere to be seen, and his words have perhaps begun to fade in their minds. Now the disciples are in charge, and a few are itching to call down the fire and brimstone. Which of the twelve sets that important precedent — death as punishment for sin — that later proves to be quite a popular theme in Christendom? Take a guess.

An elderly couple named Ananias and Sapphira, members of the infant Christian community, sell their land in order to give money to the disciples. But they also surreptitiously withhold some of it for their own use. Peter hears about this duplicity, and his judgment is immediate. He confronts them one at a time, and they die in succession. It looks for all the world like he literally scares them to death. To feeble and mourning Sapphira Peter says "Listen! At the door are the footsteps of those who have buried your husband. They will carry you out too!" The woman drops dead at his feet.

When you read Luke's two narratives in succession this comes as an horrific turn of events: two appalling deaths, a punishment that dwarfs its crime, and a near-complete repudiation of Jesus of Nazareth and all that he taught. Here the contrast between the two close friends is brought to a most terrible resolution. In the gospel Jesus treats money with complete indifference. In Acts Peter behaves as if it's deathly important. In the gospel Jesus insists that one should not tempt the Spirit. In Acts Peter calls upon it to perform his hateful will (right after accusing the old couple of having "tested the Spirit of the Lord"). In the gospel Jesus sits Peter down and carefully teaches him about the redemptive power of forgiveness. By Acts Peter has forgotten. He could not have miscounted: he was 489 short.

After this, says Luke, "a great fear came upon the whole church." But they were more than just afraid. Now they were Petrified.

IV

DEATH AND TAXES

And Caiphas was in his own Mind
A benefactor to Mankind.

"The Everlasting Gospel"

LOOKING BACK at how poorly his disciples understand Jesus, we may not want to be so harsh in judging our own failures as we try to come to terms with the man and his message. And it's not all our fault anyway — Jesus himself has to take much of the credit or blame for our continued confusion and disagreement. The man is purposefully elusive. He carefully chooses the terms of his engagements in the gospels, says things that somehow reveal and conceal him at the same time, and assiduously avoids labels of all kinds, insisting again and again that he not be given this name or that title, even bristling at benign monikers like "Nazarene." Jesus is certainly interested in "who... people say that I am," but refuses to dispel the mystery himself. This creates a tension that builds slowly as his public ministry progresses. The crowds finally become frustrated by his strange reticence on this most important question. "How long will you keep us in suspense?" they ask. Apparently a while longer.

Who do people say that he is? Some say he's "a prophet like one of the prophets of old," by which they may mean only that he's shabbily dressed and hard to manage. He is often called "Rabbi" by those who come for conversation or debate, and this title feels closer than most. He deals with the issues rabbis usually address, and sometimes teaches in the Temple with them. Like other rabbis, Jesus draws often from the Torah and the books of the prophets — by one count he quotes 87 different passages from these ancient texts (though the locals aver that "he has never studied"). The Jewish authorities at first consider him a disciple of his cousin John, and with good cause. He meets Peter and Andrew in a circle of John's followers. He doesn't begin his ministry until John has been imprisoned. Jesus' early pronouncements — "the kingdom of heaven is at hand" — are John's as well. After the Baptizer is executed Herod openly worries that Jesus is "John whose head I cut off; he is risen from the dead."

Still, none of these three titles quite fits. Jesus tells the disciples that they should call no one, not even him, "Rabbi." He does obliquely refer to himself as "prophet" once or twice, but sees himself as more than just that, as he calls John "more than a prophet." And John himself makes clear that Jesus isn't one of his disciples. So the choices continue to narrow.

At least the gospels do a good job of illustrating what Jesus *isn't*. He's not a Zealot or a militant of any stripe — he disdains all use of force and arms. He's not an Essene — he loves eating and drinking and the company of others, and spurns the traditional ascetic lifestyle. He's certainly not a Sadducee, the ultra-conservative and legalistic priests who lobby Pilate for his execution.

Strange to say, Jesus seems to fit in with the Pharisees better than any other group. As a child I was taught that Jesus and the Pharisees were always bitter enemies. But read the gospels and you'll find that his relationship with them is far more complex and interesting. Sometimes it's quite cordial; the Pharisees often have kind words for Jesus. They call him "Rabbi," "wise," and "true," "a teacher come from God." They even warn him to flee an area when Herod threatens his life. Jesus in turn instructs his followers to "do whatever they tell you and listen to what they say," since they "occupy the chair of Moses." On one occasion a leader of the Pharisees invites Jesus to his house for a meal and conversation, and he gladly accepts the offer. (Though himself something of a north-country bumpkin, Jesus never disdains the company of the urban elite. He's a friend to wealthy Pharisees like Nicodemus, and apparently even to Joseph of Arimathea, a member of the Jewish high council.)

The doctrinal parallels also are many, and help explain why a good number of the first converts to the young church are Pharisees (including Paul, and Jesus' brother James). Like the Pharisees, Jesus believes in a loving Father who will bring his children resurrection and eternal life. Like them, he scorns animal sacrifice. Like them, he preaches an ethical code that transcends all other loyalties, even loyalty to country. Like them, he believes that the children of Abraham are sent as a blessing for all peoples of the earth. A number of his specific lessons are similar to ones commonly taught by Pharisees, and reinforce their Talmudic principles.

But Jesus' differences with the Pharisees are just as striking. He prefers poetic modes of expression; they rely on logical argument. He refuses to support many of the traditional tenets of Judaic religious doctrine. He has a bad habit of breaking their beloved religious laws, including those governing behavior on the Sabbath. He denounces all professional religious groups, of which the Pharisees are the largest, for the prestige and wealth they accrue by virtue of their positions (a reproach that offends them grievously). And he conducts his ministry among those people that the Pharisees have written off as lazy, dirty, profane, and generally hopeless.

This last one turns out to be the most crucial difference of all. The "poor" constitute a broad segment of society that includes shepherds and prostitutes, beggars and day laborers, fishermen and itinerant craftsmen and a great variety of the immigrant, homeless, harried, diseased, and disabled. These are people who live precariously, who eat what they earn each day, who in war or famine are the first to die. They're accustomed to insult and injury, plagued by frustration, anxiety, and disease, disdained by civil authority, deprived even of the hope or consolation of religious faith. They are the ones the Pharisees call "the rabble, who know nothing of the law," and whom Jesus calls "the poor in spirit." They simply don't have the time or money or disposition to observe properly the intricate and resource-consuming practices of orthodox Judaism. (Fasting is a sacred act, you see; starving is a profane one.) Most of them can't even read the holy books, the great code of the Jewish faith. The verdict is unhappy but, in the Pharisees' judgment, inevitable: "They are damned."

Jesus, undaunted, molds and directs his teachings to this most common denomination. It's clear early in the gospels just how much sympathy he feels for their itinerant souls: "He had compassion on them, because they were harassed and helpless, like sheep without a shepherd." Jesus' preaching is directed most specifically to the poor. He speaks less often in the synagogues than on the hills and by the sea. And he introduces a simple and intimate style of prayer in place of the overwrought liturgical productions of the scribes, which he calls efforts of "pretense," or those of the pagans, "who think their gods will hear them because their prayers are long." The prayer he teaches his disciples is an excellent example of his preferred diction and syntax — straightforward, short, and earnest, composed more of verbs than nouns, focusing more on actions than on abstract ideas. Jesus speaks "with authority," but not *as* authority. Most of the time he speaks in parables, sketches about common events in people's lives, where the ruckus created by neighbors keeps you up at night, a lost coin puts a family in a state of panic, stewards cheat on their accounts, farmers sow their seed before ploughing, and the poor bury their money deep in the earth for safekeeping. Jesus knows this world. He lives as a peasant, and his teachings reflect peasant concerns. You would pray for daily bread only if you had doubts about getting it. His injunction to "not be anxious about tomorrow" addresses this anxiety. If you are struck on the cheek, he says, don't strike back — a teaching for people used to being struck. It is Jesus who coins the evocative phrase "salt of the earth." These are his people: "the meek," "those who mourn," "who labor and are heavy laden," who "hunger and thirst for righteousness."

Where Jesus sees a promise to be fulfilled the Pharisees see a problem to be avoided. The poor are a theological problem because they can never *hope* to fulfill the rigid demands of the law. And they're a political problem because those who have least to lose are first to question the established order of things. The Pharisees are bound to maintain that order, and not just because they love their lives of privilege. They are also deeply devoted to the preservation of Judaism. For many years they've been key to its continuance, walking a skillful line between the Roman authorities on the one hand and the Jewish "rabble" on the other. Any new teaching or idea in the heads of the volatile peasantry threatens the uneasy symbiosis of power that keeps the Jewish state intact, and any leader of the poor is a potential threat to that order. The Pharisees are obviously worried that Jesus will become the latest in that long line of fanatics who stirred up peasant animosity against the occupying forces of Rome. Many charismatics, magicians, bandits, and self-proclaimed kings in the past had done just that, leaving Palestine with a legacy of burned villages, crucified elders, and enslaved townspeople. Only a generation earlier another Galilean, named Judas, had led a religious revolt against Roman taxation — an unpleasant episode mentioned in the book of Acts. Judas had called cowards those Jews who "after serving God, accepted human masters"; for his pains he and his followers were slaughtered in the desert, and many innocents were later punished or executed. The Pharisees want to know if Jesus offers more of the same. So they ask him, a little artlessly: "Do we pay taxes to Caesar or not?"

The difference in approaches is evident from the start. The Pharisees deal in the abstract and general; Jesus prefers the concrete and particular. He asks for a coin. The emperor's head is clearly embossed on one side, but Jesus plays the country clod. "Whose head is this?" he asks. Caesar's, they reply, perhaps feeling foolish at having to answer a foolish question. Now the rustic makes his discovery. The owner put his likeness on his own coin! It belongs to Mr. Caesar.

Jesus takes a momentous political issue, over which many have fought and died, and makes a joke of it. Instead of a life-and-death matter he sees no matter at all. This response "took them by surprise"; rather than an immediate retort, there is only a caesura. In sharp contrast to Judas the Galilean, Jesus maintains that the temporal and eternal authorities are not really in competition at all. Money really *does* belong to Caesar, whoever he happens to be that year. (All currency is property of the Empire, and can't be destroyed, under penalty of law.) So a coin makes a fitting "tribute" to him, who deserves no less, and no more. But it's of no real consequence. What matters is not what you give to Caesar, Jesus concludes, but what you give to God. And what does God require? Only yourself. The coin bears the likeness of Caesar, and therefore should go to Caesar. But people, he sometimes reminds his listeners, bear the likeness of God.

Let's not overlook the unique basis of Jesus' approach to this issue, too easily done with a story we may have heard a thousand times. He focuses on the question of *values*, which is the antecedent to the Pharisees' facile question of *loyalties*. "Where your treasure is," Jesus sums up in one excellent phrase, "there will your heart be also." Apparently he sees, not a perversion of loyalties, but a perversion of values in the religious class, whose members he says "like to walk about in long robes," "take the place of honor at feasts," and claim that "if someone swears by the Temple it is nothing, but he is bound by his oath if he swears by its gold."

Of course, they're not alone in this opinion. Such is the general understanding of Pharisee and fisherman alike: it's money that matters. Paying taxes to Caesar means giving to him a thing of great value that rightly belongs to God. Jesus considers this a laughable stance, and his reply to the Pharisees is flippant. But his root objection is deadly serious. It's that money *doesn't* matter — and that no one seems to know what a truly valuable thing is. "What is highly esteemed in human eyes," he solemnly states, "is detestable in God's sight."

Throughout his brief ministry Jesus shows little interest in matters of money. He pays no mind to the financial dealings of his shifty treasurer (coincidentally, another money-obsessed peasant named Judas). He never gives alms to the poor. He refuses to arbitrate between two men contesting an inheritance. He cares not at all that the fine oil a woman uses to cleanse and anoint him was very expensive. When Jesus does mention money he turns its face value upside down: in his stories money isn't treated even as a dependable measure of *material* value. Think of the parable of the talents, of the dishonest steward, of the laborers who worked all day in a vineyard. The monetary values here are skewed, and our first reaction is that someone has been treated unfairly. How can a servant with one talent be expected to do as much, or even obtain the same interest rate, as someone with five? How can a steward who cheats his master on his accounts be commended by him for prudence? How can a vineyard owner pay the same amount for an hour's and a day's work? Consider Jesus' remark about the widow, whose gift of two copper coins he says is greater than the large sums contributed by wealthy men. He insists that a tiny amount of money, a really insignificant amount, is of more importance, of greater *value*, than a much larger contribution. As Blake says:

> *The poor Man's farthing is worth more*
> *Than all the Gold on Africs Shore.*

The old woman's contribution has nothing to do with the

market price of copper. It bears no relation to "value" as it's generally understood. Jesus is positing the presence of some other standard of value, one not visible, and certainly not quantifiable, and therefore not often acknowledged by those around him.

This discussion of standards of value continues when the Sadducees step up — they who don't believe in life after death — and pose for Jesus a second puzzler. A woman had seven husbands on earth, they say, marrying each brother in succession when his elder sibling passed away, just as Moses instructed us to do. "In the resurrection, to which of the seven will she be wife?" Of course the Sadducees aren't really interested in a solution to a situation so hypothetical. They just want to create as many logical difficulties for resurrectionists as they themselves have in believing in only this one life, where it rains on the just and unjust in equal measure. So Jesus' reply is curt and cutting: "You don't know either the scriptures or the power of God." Your values and assumptions make no sense, he argues, when you transfer them to the realm of the eternal. There people are "like angels," so a question about marriage in heaven is like a question about its sewage treatment system — it's foolish and empty.

Here again Jesus points to the true source of the apparently insoluble quandaries presented by these lawyers, priests, and moral bureaucrats. Their approach, their understandings and values and beliefs grow out of earth's own clay. *Of course* the Sadducees don't believe in a resurrection: they can believe only in what tradition and experience tell them. That means a reliance on religious law and natural law, on language and sense, on arbitrary distinctions and measurements like money and time and weight and distance. Consider their Sabbath laws. You can have a fire, but not light one. You can swallow vinegar, but not gargle it. You can walk three-eighths of a mile, but not half a mile. But there are no miles in an eternal realm, no time, no money, no marriage. And no death either, Jesus tells them: "God is not God of the dead, but of the living." He wants them to understand that *all* human contracts, measurements, judgments, and distinctions — even our most beloved, like marriage — are contingent and conditional. They pass away in the presence of eternity.

Another example. The Pharisees criticize Jesus and his disciples for eating without first washing their hands. Disregard for this basic ritual offends them because it violates the "tradition of the elders." (They themselves "never eat without washing their arms as far as the elbow.") It also indicates once again that this rednecked fringe element is dangerous, a threat to law and order. And of course it is — in this case, to the law and order represented by the Pharisees themselves, who uphold a religious and moral standard for the nation. Jesus claims that it isn't a standard worth having, grounded as it is in human values: "How ingeniously you get round the commandments of God in order to preserve your own tradition!" What you do, you do not for God, but to satisfy yourselves. Clean hands are of no real value to God, says Jesus. Cleanliness for him is an inward and spiritual matter. Only in the gospels according to *us* is it external (and perfectly summed up in the inane Protestant proverb "Cleanliness is next to godliness").

Jesus explains all of this very carefully: "Hear me, all of you, and understand: there is nothing outside a man which by going into him can defile him [(since, as he notes elsewhere, food "enters, not his heart, but his stomach")]; the things which come *out* of a man are what defile him." It's a strange value structure, he points out, that equates dirt and sweat with "murder, adultery, fornication, theft... " The Pharisees can make this equation because they are interested only in the outward and visible, in "the outside of cup and dish," in what women and men appear to be, and not what they are. And "they have their reward" — superb hygiene.

Why are the Pharisees so obsessed with outward behavior?

Jesus suggests that it stems from their devotion to the law, the conceptual groundwork of their lives. He argues, *scandalously*, that law is an external measure that encourages people to concern themselves with outward things, behaviors evident to the world, and to ignore what they inwardly are. So the Pharisees can observe the tiny rituals and prohibitions of daily Jewish life as law and tradition dictate, and still harbor mean and selfish spirits within. They "tithe mint and dill and cumin," Jesus says, and neglect "justice and mercy and faith." They concern themselves with appearances, and not with truths. He compares them to "whitewashed tombs" that are clean and white on the outside, "but inside are full of dead men's bones." "Hypocrites!" he shouts at them, capping one such diatribe. (The disciples later warn Jesus that the Pharisees "took offense" at what he said, not understanding that this was his intention.)

Because law is external, it's easily put to selfish purposes — to secure individual salvation, protect material rights and possessions, justify one's behavior and manner of living, convince others of one's worthiness and thereby lead to political power and social prestige. Jesus says this is exactly what the Pharisees do: "You are those who justify yourselves in the sight of others." And yet the great irony here, he points out, is that law doesn't justify people at all! It *condemns* them. Everyone falls short before the law, he says. All men and women are imperfect, and fail to keep God's commandments: "Did not Moses give you the law? Yet none of you keeps the law." Law is absolute and unwavering in its denunciation of *all* people as transgressors. And "not one iota" of it can pass away.

Since all have sinned, Jesus wonders aloud why any one person would blame another for a failure to observe the law. How can I condemn the spot I think I see in my neighbor's eye when my own is so blocked up? My imperfections call into question the veracity of my judgment. And the judgment itself then serves to make my own sins appear all the more unpardonable! So Jesus recommends that people avoid being condemned simply by not condemning others. In an astounding conceptual coup, he applies the fundamental principle of law — reciprocity — to law itself. In this way he attempts to break the vicious circle of sin and condemnation and guilt once and for all.

This new approach has never been seen or heard before, and when Jesus suggests it the reaction is always stunned silence. Consider the dramatic scene that takes place shortly after the Pharisees catch a woman in the act of adultery. They intend to stone her, meting out a punishment that dates back to the days of Moses, and clearly prescribed in the book of Deuteronomy: "In this way thou shalt put away evil from among you." But when they see Jesus they decide to use the situation to its fullest. They leave it to him either to condemn the adulteress to this brutal end or break with the great lawgiver himself. The woman is cowering in the middle of a mob apparently ready to perform this horrendous method of execution. Her shame and her terror can only be imagined, and she can hardly hide either, there "in the midst" for everyone to see. Jesus appears unmoved by the scene though, and when the Pharisees first speak he acts "as if he had not heard them." He squats on the ground and doodles strangely with his finger in the dirt (never clean!). His response, when it finally comes, is terse: "Let the one without sin be the first to throw a stone at her." He then goes back to writing on the ground.

Jesus doesn't deny that the woman is a sinner who deserves death. The reply seems to suggest that she does. His only question is who will judge that sin and execute its penalty. Here is the point — that only a *perfect* person can judge imperfection. And from the perspective of perfection, this woman is hardly more or less sinful than anyone else! The Jews think adultery is nearly as terrible as murder. But Jesus says that either you're a sinner or you're not. Everyone has sinned. And all sinners deserve death. The Pharisees claim that he, and everyone standing around, has the legal right, even the obligation, to crush her skull with rocks. Jesus replies that in the face of perfection legal right passes away. But his manner is oddly off-hand, the anticlimax almost comic. The Pharisees and their crowd, "beginning with the eldest," slink away, like guilty things, until only two remain. "Where are your accusers?" the man finally asks the woman. "Has no one condemned you?" She says no one has; he says he doesn't either.

Please note one final irony. Jesus says that he "and the Father are one." And "the Father," who is perfect, *has* judged, and has rightly condemned to death, by stone, fire, and sword, vast multitudes of sinful people. Jesus claims to act on behalf of this God, the one being who really is without sin. But he doesn't pick up that first fatal stone (though he does crouch on the ground among them, probably too close for the woman's comfort). The Hand of God was once justly raised in anger to smite the unrighteous. Now it remains low, drawing strange pictures in the dust.

V

FINITE AND INFINITE

If the doors of perception were cleansed, everything would appear to man as it is, infinite. For man has closed himself up, til he sees all things thro' narrow chinks of his cavern.

"The Marriage of Heaven and Hell"

WHAT DO ALL of these encounters between Jesus and his disciples, and Jesus and the Pharisees, have in common? Just this: in each the parties disagree about what is valuable, and what is real. But let's dig down, if we can, to the root of their contention. The words "real" and "valuable" aren't much help by themselves, since they've been used to signify so much, and change their meanings to suit the occasion. Jesus addresses a great variety of issues, but his approach is the same each time. It's an approach rooted in what he believes to be the crucial distinction implicit in all life: the distinction between *finite* and *infinite*. For Jesus, the things of real value are the things that are boundless and eternal — infinite. Coins and temples are not valuable. Only a thing that can last forever is valuable. Even marriage, and sin, he maintains, aren't real. They pass away. Nothing that is finite is certain, says Jesus: not even death and taxes.

The man is clearly a radical — in the literal sense of the word. "Radical" (like "radish") comes from the Latin "*radix*," meaning "root." Radical ideas come from the root, the basis, the fundamentals of life. They're the source and foundation of everything above them. The prophetic call is always a "radical" call to repentance, to "turn back" to the source, to that which is eternal and unchanging. For Jesus, as for the prophets before him, only the most "radical" matters, those of "your immortal soul," are worthy of close attention and concern. Wealth is certainly not important, nor is social prestige, nor what you eat, nor how you dress. Whatever is mortal or transitory is at root valueless. So Jesus exhorts his listeners, day after day, in subtle and not-so-subtle ways, to free themselves from mundane preoccupations with hygiene and finances and politics, as well as from general worry about the past and future, which he says leads only to "dissipation" and "anxiousness" about "the cares of this life." "Do not be afraid," he counsels. Don't burden yourselves with never-ending concerns over food and clothing. Look at the birds. Consider the lilies. Ask only for bread for the day at hand: "Each day has enough troubles of its own." In the realm of the infinite there is only one day, where what you do is what you are. Fear God only, and man not at all. Forget what you have been, however upright or iniquitous. Your past is gone, the future is never, and the present requires one thing of everyone. So live in the Eternal Now.

More than simply strange, Jesus' perspective is broader than that adopted by his fellow Jews, embracing values that fall outside the limits of a single life span. By sharing it he intends to force in his listeners a radical re-thinking of the motives and purposes for their actions and beliefs. Why place your hopes on a building that will crumble, he asks them? Why judge one person when all are imperfect? Why fight the Roman Empire when it will fall on its own? Why "worry and fret about so many things" when "yet few are needed, indeed only one"? Why worry about tomorrow when tomorrow never comes? (Why indeed? From this angle Jesus' reputed "idealism" begins to look downright pragmatic.)

A word to the wise, though: this kind of re-thinking puts us on perilous ground, near the real roots of our being, stripped of our fabricated flooring. Many of our most cherished enterprises may be called into question, as well as their motives and goals. The great Danish philosopher Soren Kierkegaard writes that the "collision of the finite and the infinite... is precisely a mortal danger for one who is composed of both," but that's just the collision Jesus wants to engineer.

◆   ◆   ◆

His distinction between "finite" and "infinite" is the foundation of Jesus' value system, and the radical cause of all the problems we've had with understanding and believing the man in the first place. Most importantly, it explains why many of his teachings are so offensive to us: they challenge the validity of our most beloved and deeply inbred values. Over the ages we've tended to assume without question that he endorses them, since most seem to us absolutely right and honorable. But Jesus often shocks people by claiming that their values are finite, that they're of human rather than divine origin, that "what you do you do not for God, but for man." And this includes values expressed in devotion to moral law, to religious observance, to country and family! These are often not noble or admirable at all, he says, since they're really designed to serve our selfish needs. The teachings we revere as sacred law Jesus calls "nothing but human commandments." Could any attack on our lives and values be more "radical," or more offensive, than this?

This crucial distinction also explains why we find the *form* of Jesus' words and ideas so difficult and confusing. He is trying to get finite language to express infinite ideas. He wants to do the impossible — to describe infinity. And he does in fact give it a name: "the kingdom of God" or "the kingdom of heaven." These are terms of his and his cousin's devising; you won't find either anywhere in the Old Testament. (The finite realm Jesus usually just calls "the world.") He knows he has to use a human tool to describe the infinite, and he is well aware of the debilitating limits of language. For this reason Jesus always says what the kingdom of heaven is "like" rather than what it "is." For this reason he sticks to symbol and story. But he treats these as opportunities rather than obstacles. We've already looked at many of the ways Jesus bends and stretches language in ways it has never been bent or stretched before. Suffice it here to repeat that, in his efforts, finite grammars are sometimes wrecked altogether: "Before Abraham was, I Am."

The grammar and semantics of finite thinking, its operating machinery, and the claims it makes about "the world," are what Jesus tries to call into question. In this connection he demonstrates not only the frailties of language but of sense experience as well. Jesus remarks often on the failures of sense: that people can "look without seeing, and listen without hearing or understanding." Our five senses manage to conceal as much about the finite world as they reveal, so the conclusions we draw about the world based on their data are untrustworthy. This is probably why Jesus warns his disciples not to be impressed by miracle, but instead to base their faith on something more real than the telecast of their senses. His simple recommendation is that people "not judge according to appearances," as the Pharisees do.

Our devotion to sense is easily explained — we love the immediate, finite world we inhabit, the one under our dominion, within which "man is the measure of all things," and therefore we're devoted to the sensory apparatus that bring us that world, in however fragmentary a fashion. Sense tends to suggest that this tangible, visible, tastable, quasi-controllable world is all that really is, or at least all that really matters. There can be no sensory window on the infinite, since "what is flesh is flesh, and what is Spirit is Spirit." (Of God Jesus baldly tells his listeners "His voice you have never heard, his form you have never seen.") We're unable to understand or assert our control over an infinite realm, so it's not surprising that we might prefer our own, and simply ignore the "radical" questions, those of spirit and truth. But Jesus wants at least to call to his listeners' attention their act of willful blindness.

> *This Life's dim Windows of the Soul*
> *Distorts the Heavens from Pole to Pole*
> *And leads you to believe a Lie*
> *When you see with, not thro', the Eye*

Again it is William Blake, one of the gospels' closest readers, who ploughs this difficult epistemological field for us. Blake spells out the problems with reliance on sense, and on the empirical method in general, hinted at but not fully articulated by Jesus. Living at the apex of what even today we happily call "The Enlightenment," he enumerates the assumptions of empiricism (and its theology, Deism) and explodes them in two contrary series of aphorisms entitled "There Is No Natural Religion."

In the first series Blake outlines the precepts of empirical philosophy ("Man cannot naturally Percieve but through his natural or bodily organs") in order to reflect on the reductive nature of sense and its failure even to come to proper terms with itself: "From a perception of only 3 senses or 3 elements none could deduce a fourth or fifth." This is a fatal finite flaw, so deep that we can't even experience it as a limitation! Such impediments to our understanding are severe: "The desires & perceptions of man, untaught by anything but organs of sense, must be limited to objects of sense." But we may actually *prefer* these impediments, too comfortable with them to let them go now, addicted to a world that's knowable, definable, and humanly controllable. Blake notes that the empirical model makes of this world and our lives "a dull round" from which there is no escape. But at least it's *our* dull round.

With his second series of aphorisms Blake presents the precepts of faith and revelation, the impossible apprehension of the infinite. "Man's perceptions are not bounded by organs of perception; he percieves more than sense (tho' ever so acute) can discover." Such an absurd statement can hardly be proved, but that's just what commends it to Blake. It's an impossible Truth waiting to be seen — but through a spiritual seeing not accomplished by our eyes. When we use this other mode of apprehension we soon realize that the dull round of reason and sense can never satisfy the human spirit: "The bounded is loathed by its possessor." And when we begin to explore our hearts it occurs to us that "the desire of Man [is] Infinite," which means that man "is... himself Infinite." This is at the scandalous heart of what Jesus wants to convey to his followers, and Blake sums it up superbly: "He who sees the Infinite in all things, sees God. He who sees the Ratio only, sees himself only. Therefore God becomes as we are, that we may be as he is."

Once we're confronted with the failure of sense, and its step-child knowledge, we may be ready to try faith, to reach out beyond what's definable, manageable, quantifiable, finite. Only through faith can we imagine a Truth that lies beyond this world's dense atmosphere. Otherwise we're grounded, left only with what Blake calls "the Ratio" between all perceptible things, and eventually become inured to that same dull round, the vicious circle within which faith can find no foothold. "How can you believe," Jesus asks a group of Pharisees, "since you look to *one another* for approval?" Before the faculty of faith can be exercised we have to break that cycle of self-referentiality, the idolatrous chasing after the works of human hands, our craven dependence on sense and on human constructs like logic and language and law, our morbid reliance on the arbitrary but deeply ingrained "precepts of men."

Our spirits yearn to be liberated; our egos suppress the craving. Jesus is condemned by the religious classes for wanting to break out of the dull round of reason, to offer something more than just himself and the apprehensible world, to point beyond himself and it, to teach an infinite message instead of a finite one. Isn't that the whole purpose of a religious faith? You would think so. But the Pharisees oppose him in this anyway. It's as if they embrace their religion in order to subvert its chief aim —

communion with God — and keep things solely within their tiny circle of influence. Despite what they say, the Pharisees "love human glory more than the glory of God." The stark irony of their position astonishes Jesus: "If someone should come in his *own* name you would accept him!" Of course they would. Only the name of God could threaten their dominion.

In contrast to the Pharisees, Jesus teaches that the finite can and should be pierced with infinity. He claims that the infinite can take on the form of the finite. Then he begins to teach, by word and action, that he is that form, or an example of that form. He heals people of sickness (though others ask "who gave [him] authority to act like this?"). He forgives sins ("who can forgive sins but God alone?"). He performs a number of apparently miraculous acts (to marvel "that such powers were given to human beings"). He even "calls God his own Father, making himself equal to God." He says the parallel lines of finitude and infinity can meet, and cross each other: "You will see heaven opened, and the angels of God ascending and descending upon the Son of Man." In fact, Jesus claims godhead for *all* the daughters and sons of man. He says that the power of infinity is now readily available to every human being, so that his followers will perform even greater feats than he has! People can now forgive sins. They can heal. They are masters of the Sabbath, and "greater than the Temple." The Pharisees want to stone him for saying such things. Jesus confronts them with — what else? — the *text!* "Is it not written in your Law: "I said, 'You are gods'"? And scripture cannot be broken."

♦   ♦   ♦

Perhaps we agree that what Jesus teaches is at odds with the beliefs and understandings of those around him. Maybe we think his values differ from those of people down through the centuries who have called themselves Christians. Maybe we even agree on the "root" of that difference: that Jesus espouses infinite values, ones that transcend the standards established by tradition. But we've been talking in broad terms mostly, and dwelling more on form than content; now we need to consider the specific standards of human value. What are they? And what does Jesus say about them? Here we may finally part company — with each other and with Jesus. There are plenty of toes to step on when we begin to consider the actual values that guide our lives, and we can be easily offended by the suggestion that our ideals are selfish or illusory. But Jesus says it's important to know where our real treasures lie. The question shouldn't be avoided.

It seems to me that there are three fundamental value structures at the root of human society. One is money, another, power, a third, law. In "advanced" cultures these three are carefully organized and regulated by specific agencies: the institutions of finance, politics, and justice. All find idealized expression in the great abstract structures that are said to underpin human social organization: capital, history, and morality. All three are closely interrelated. None is a discrete entity — if you have money, for instance, a kind of power is at your disposal. All three are susceptible to measurement and control — they can be quantified and portioned out systematically. All three grow naturally out of human experience. But now they govern the terms of that experience entirely.

PART III

VI

THE OLD JERUSALEM

*True Christian Charity [is] not dependent on Money...
that is, on Caesar or Empire or Natural Religion.*

"The Laocoon"

A FEW YEARS ago I was browsing in a bookstore and picked up a short novel, attracted by its brightly-colored spine. The back cover featured a blurb about its author, a black minister who had devoted his early career to working among the poor in small churches in Mississippi. He sounded like an interesting and unusual man, and he had chosen an intriguing premise for his first work of fiction: Jesus and Peter appear in our day and live among members of a rural black Baptist church. A bold conceit for a novel, I thought, and a great opportunity to reflect on how Jesus speaks to the needs and concerns of people in our own day. Stories almost always do a better job than systematic theologies at expressing the teachings of the Nazarene. I bought the novel and took it home.

The narrator explains the story's setting carefully at the start. The people of this church have been disenfranchised from their larger society. They are downtrodden and underrepresented; they hunger and thirst for righteousness. They're a faithful and kind-hearted lot, to be sure, but find themselves floundering in the world, lacking much in the way of resource or direction, desperately in need of some kind of salvation. Onto this scene Jesus and Peter arrive, *ex machina*, and move in and live among these people as two of their own. And by what fruits do they come to be known? What redemption do they offer the faithful people of God? Cash. At novel's end Jesus gives them money, and things start to look up. The narrator closes by summarizing the content of these poor folk's salvation: "a piece of the economic pie."

Maybe you're not surprised by this, or upset by the story's resolution. You certainly can't call this preacher-turned-novelist an apostate. He follows in one of the oldest human traditions — that of associating spiritual and material values. It was not a coincidence that the calf worshipped by the Israelites in the Sinai was cast of gold, or that Solomon adorned the great Temple with marvelous treasures. The Israelites understood that no material object could truly represent Yahweh, but precious metals and jewels suggested to them a richness of spirit all the same, and this facile association, over the prophets' protests, eventually congealed into religious dogma. By Jesus' day almost all Jews, the poor and the rich alike, saw wealth as a spiritual as well as a secular currency. The Pharisees, according to Jesus, taught that an oath offered on the Temple's gold was more binding than an oath on the Temple itself! Financial success they always interpreted as a clear indication of God's blessing. For the Pharisees, material and spiritual wealth weren't rivals. They actually *guaranteed* one another — otherwise one couldn't break the cycle of material and spiritual poverty to which "the rabble" were so hopelessly consigned. Good Jews had to muster considerable resources in order to observe the rituals and devotions of their faith. And only by means of such expensive and time-consuming devotions could they be blessed with a prosperous life. This may sound like more of Blake's "dull round," but the Pharisees, who Luke says "loved money," could imagine no other mechanics of salvation. Even many novelists can't do that.

And neither could the early Christian church. You might think that after their unhappy experience with their first treasurer, and after Jesus' indifference to the office, the disciples would be skittish about re-establishing it. They were not: a collection of funds was one of their first orders of business. The willingness of others to give freely to the new movement was taken as the measure of their devotion (just ask Sapphira), and the swelling of church coffers was interpreted as a sign of God's blessing. Thus the Judeo-Christian economic tradition began strong, and grew through the years. You have probably heard all the usual examples, like the practice of buying "indulgences," monetary gifts to the church that were vaguely understood to improve one's relationship with God. The finest symbol of this tradition is the popular medieval crucifix depicting Jesus with one hand nailed to the cross and the other firmly grasping a purse ceintured to his waist. Over the ages many questioned this belief in the redemptive value of lucre, but most opposition was effectively squelched. In some instances Christians who insisted on the poverty of Jesus, and who renounced all material possessions themselves, were burned at the stake.

In this respect the Reformation, which is supposed to have developed partly in response to the "selling out" of the church, offered no reform at all. In fact, Calvinism and other doctrinal systems escalated the pursuit of mammon to frenetic levels by insisting that prosperity is an emblem of divine election — that those whom God favors and elects to eternal life, he blesses with material wealth. This teaching turned out to be just the psychological impetus needed to fuel the engines of advanced capitalism. Protestant theology became a singular inspiration to the development of complex financial systems, free-market economics, and western-style affluence in general, and Christians have since devoted astounding energies to spreading an ethic of hard work, consumerism, and material success.

It should be noted, though, that the Christian preoccupation with wealth doesn't spring from purely selfish motives. Certainly no world institution has been more giving of its money than the Christian church, and no people more generous than its members. Religious westerners have always believed that financial giving is a good thing, and for two reasons: it helps others, and it leads to receiving. Giving to others leaves them a specific material benefit that will improve the quality of their lives, allow them to reverse the cycle of material and spiritual poverty that so oppresses them. And that same material benefit may be the giver's as well. What goes around comes around. You get as you give.

These are the two founding principles of spiritual economics, of Prosperity Theology, and they boast many devotees on the left and the right. Even to atheists and agnostics they appear right and reasonable, as beautifully congruent as Newton's laws of motion. Certainly their usefulness in society, both as a corollary to the "work ethic" and as a powerful sales pitch, commend them well enough. In Christian churches, for example, the faithful are often exhorted to "plant a seed of faith" by making financial contributions to those doing God's work, whether at the local, national, or international level. Such gifts are touted as investments that can grow and return to the giver, perhaps many times over. This has been the teaching of medieval pardoner and modern parson, and it has loosened purse strings for centuries. The pardoner sold (appropriately enough) Peter's bones. The modern parson has his own strategies. Today some mainline Protestant churches offer money-back guarantees: if you don't receive a "blessing" within ninety days of your contribution, it will be refunded.

Recently I watched a paid television broadcast in which an evangelist was soliciting donations from his audience. He drew close to the camera and read a letter he'd received from a middle-aged single mother. She wrote to tell him that she needed a car. She had worked hard her whole life, sometimes held down two or three jobs at once, and always tried to do what she thought was right in pursuit of the American Dream. But for some reason things hadn't worked out. Her husband deserted her two months ago; right now she could barely feed the kids. If she could get hold of a car, though, she was *sure* that things would change for the better. The woman enclosed a small check to the evangelist to secure it for her, and he held up the check for his audience to see, his thumb over the woman's name. Then, his voice rising, he said that Satan himself had kept that car from her, and wouldn't let it go. But what was Jesus going to do? He was going to free that car up. *Free it up!* he shouted, so that the mother could get it. He could see it, even now: a Ford Fairmont.

Most of us call this kind of scene a transparent ruse, doubly appalling because it victimizes those who can least afford it. A sick ploy, we say. She'll never see that car. The woman is never going to get what she needs to turn her life around. She'll be even more helpless after this than she was before, and the preacher will be that much better off.

Our opprobrium falls short of its mark. In truth what we share with that sad preacher is more significant than what we don't. We unquestioningly embrace his short-sighted vision of the world, equally immersed in it as we are. The logic of our attitude proclaims that a car really *is* what that woman needs, and that if someone could deliver one he would be a good and righteous man, a model disciple of the Nazarene. The legacy of Pharisee and disciple is as evident today as ever: we believe we're blessed by God whenever there's an improvement in the material conditions of our lives. According to one recent survey, 71% of Americans believe that their financial status reflects how God feels about them.

This idea, and many others of its kind, survives only by means of a careful avoidance of the gospels. There Jesus consistently works to strip wealth of its sacramental character, to deny that it offers in itself a valuable ministry to others, or provides them with what they most need. In itself, he says, money is "a tainted thing." It can be useful only as a utensil for what really matters — the act of giving itself. This, like all sacraments, is not a *thing* but an *act*, valuable in itself, and not because of its dubious by-products. (What good is a widow's

mite to the numberless poor?) The gift Mary of Bethany gave to
Jesus, anointing his head and feet, was one such sacramental
gift, and Jesus notes that the cash value of the oil didn't matter.
Her gift was more valuable than oil, which is bought and sold
and used and lost.

Jesus *never once* mentions the material value of the work
done for people by charity, the common justification for such
efforts offered by Christians and agnostics alike. His unique
emphasis is always on the benefit to the *giver.* We often do lip
service to this sentiment, but Jesus actually appears to believe
that it's a greater blessing "to give than to receive." So what *is*
the blessing provided by giving to others? How does it enrich
us? It's hard to say. There are no miracles where Jesus turns
lead into gold. In fact, he never construes physical wealth as a
sign of blessing. He insists instead that "a man's life does not
consist in the abundance of his possessions." Not once does Jesus
suggest that his followers might gain some material advantage
by following him. He recommends instead that they give away
what little they have. He doesn't even allow praise or acclaim
for such unselfishness, since he says true giving is anonymous,
a work the right hand does on the sly. There simply isn't any
material or social reward offered. No money for your purse, no
second tunic for your wardrobe, maybe not even a certificate of
commendation. So where's the blessing?

Maybe it lies in its one obvious effect. Giving to others
means you end up a little poorer. The blessing is in having a
little less of an investment in "the things of this world," so that
you can make a greater investment in the life of the spirit.
Eventually we're going to have to choose anyway, says Jesus:
"you cannot be the slave both of God and of money." And what
he calls "the lure of riches" is strong. It can easily take over our
lives, crowding out the things of real joy and lasting value.
Parable after parable illustrates this theme: we build ourselves
great storehouses and die without enjoying them; preoccupied
with our possessions, we skip the wonderful banquet to which

we've been invited.

Still, the moral imagination of Christian and atheist alike is so programmed by commercial values that we can see money as the only way to redress the world's unending grief. This may explain why the material and spiritual aspects of our lives mesh so happily in our biggest Christian holiday — and why "A Christmas Carol" is far and away the most popular parable of the twentieth century. The story is premised on the difference in values between a poor person and a rich one. The poor man's values are admirable, and the rich man's are not. But the story doesn't muster the strength of its own convictions. In its great materialist catharsis Scrooge moves to make Bob Cratchit wealthy too, and the reader breathes a stale sigh of relief. For a moment it looked as if the gift was to be another one entirely: the liberation from our slavish devotion to a world of dreary jobs and dirty florins, and an initiation into a new life of spirit that beggars the biggest turkey at the market. But we're not ready for such a complete and dramatic liberation, one that requires the total giving of self that a child in a stable represents.

Material salvation may be the only kind of salvation we can imagine, and heaven we confuse with the American Dream. I'm reminded of a recent popular movie in which the heroine is trapped in the "dead-end" job of secretary. She is frustrated by working in an atmosphere where she must call her bosses by their last names and fetch them coffee in the morning. In a wild sequence of events she manages to maneuver around these selfish people and secure a position with an office and secretary of her own. Of course, the movie is not about *that* secretary (as Dickens' tale is not about the millions of other cold and hungry Cratchits in London) — this other woman will apparently be satisfied with a position where she can call her boss by her first name and get her coffee only when she wants some herself. Surely her spirit is full. And the heroine? The camera moves back to show her new office. It is a clean and spacious place. It has a window and a view. Its door has her name on it. Music swells as the movie ends and the camera pans the room one final time. A gospel choir begins to sing: "The New Jerusalem." But of course it's the same old Jerusalem after all.

The world loves gala benefit balls, charity rock concerts, and big numbers of all kinds (though every number is finite). John D. Rockefeller, Jr. donated hundreds of millions of dollars to charities and foundations during his lifetime, and the world esteemed him a great and good man. But true philanthropists teach us otherwise. Mother Teresa visited this country a number of years back and was offered a large check for her orphanage by a wealthy Californian. She turned him down. God will provide, she said. The aspiring benefactor was shocked, and more than a little insulted. But what does he think of his money? Does he think it can solve any problem? Will it abolish poverty and hunger and misery and sickness? Those will always be with us, says Jesus. Teresa is involved in establishing a Christian community, which is funded with the pennies of widows, with the giving of self and the sacrifice that entails. Only a full human community can endure as long as the poor will endure — long after the money has run out.

This kind of approach is usually dismissed as callow idealism. It sounds very nice, the response goes, but we have to live in the real world, where single mothers live with minimum wage jobs and without transportation. I imagine this is the most common unspoken objection to Jesus' teachings: too idealistic (by which we mean "not *really* true"). But consider for a moment just whose approach is the more idealistic. Would a Ford Fairmont save that desperate woman? Is that what she most needs? Would it really turn her life around? No amount of money or vehicles, however great, can do that, and we kid ourselves daily in thinking that it could. The world provides precious little evidence to support the idea that wealth leads to a more fulfilling life, or even a superficially happier one. (Epicurus said that 2400 years ago, and him we've made into an epicure.) The pain and despondency of the rich is qualitatively different from that of the poor, but it's every bit as deep and pervasive. On some level we all know that, but our quixotic devotion to material values only grows. Belief in the redemptive power of money is the purest kind of idealism there is, a material faith contradicted by all material evidence. That single mother lives distraught and helpless and desperate. Howard Hughes died distraught and helpless and desperate. Both hoped for a material deliverance; both need another kind of deliverance altogether. We all enjoy ridiculing the lunatic preachers on television. But do we see how much we have in common with them? We all trade in the same finite currency. We too would like to be sent a car, whose commercials always promise freedom and deliverance.

We believe that our problems are material, so we're quick to seek a material solution. This is especially true of those of us on the religious left, intent upon our struggle for various forms of social and economic justice. Even these, our highest standards, often serve as a canny disguise for the same old values. I'm reminded of a prominent Protestant cleric and social activist, a man with a profound and altruistic devotion to his ideals, a devotion admirable in itself (since, as Blake notes, "many are not capable of a firm perswasion of any thing"). This single-minded dedication has led him to committing acts of civil disobedience; he has often gone to prison for what he believes. The problem is that his ideals, which at first glance seem so commendable, grow out of the very cultural values he claims to oppose, and make sense only within their context. It's a context in which every value is immediate and quantifiable, in which each can be measured and meted out like grain. The result is less than inspiring. Justice, for example, the cleric argues, is achieved "when teachers get paid as much as corporate lawyers." It's hard to imagine an ideal more paltry than that, or one less worthy of the sacrifice of our lives. It's impossible to conceive of Jesus teaching such a thing: "The kingdom of

heaven is like a man who instituted an equitable pay scale."
Jesus is concerned with another kind of poverty altogether. He
says he's sent to "the poor in spirit," and acknowledges only this
as true poverty. Would the minister really care to argue that a
poor teacher who is rich in spirit has a life inferior in quality to
that of a wealthy executive?

I once heard a speech in which an Episcopal bishop
advocated the development a new social focus for her church,
one that proceeds out of a "holistic analysis" that moves away
from treating symptoms of problems to attacking "root causes."
And what are the causes of our problems? Institutionalized
social and economic inequity. This is the real enemy, the bishop
insisted, the one that prohibits people from leading full lives.
It's the enemy we as Christians are called to fight.

But consider Jesus' work among the poor, with whom he
spends his entire ministry. He consistently treats the effects of
poverty rather than what we consider to be their root causes. He
heals the diseased, feeds the hungry, counsels the desperate
and forlorn. (Treating "effects" means dealing, not with tidy
policy, but with untidy people.) He lives with the peasantry of
Palestine, and sees what the oppression of the Romans and the
contumely of the Pharisees does to them on a daily basis. Yet
never does he suggest that the poor protest the sorry conditions
under which they live. Not once does he tell them to rise up
against the social and economic institutions that perpetuate
those conditions. The bishop is right to say that poverty will
never be eradicated Jesus' way. Jesus suggests that it will never
be eradicated at all: "The poor you will always have with you."
And yet, strangely enough, these aren't words of grim
resignation. They sound more like a promise than a threat.

Liberal Christianity continues to teach that the salvation of
the poor can come by way of a welfare system, or social
tolerance, or a particular fashion of political thinking. So it finds
it necessary to mischaracterize Jesus' teachings to the poor. But
his point is not theirs — that the poor have been denied

blessing by societies of this and every age. It's that they *are* blessed, in their present state and moment. In fact he goes further than that. Jesus insists that the poor aren't blessed in *spite* of the fact that they are impoverished and oppressed, but *because* they're impoverished and oppressed. "Blessed are you who are poor," he says. "The kingdom of heaven is yours." This is deeply offensive to a world where success is measured in currency, but it's the gospel. In the finite world, poverty and persecution are curses. In the realm of the infinite, says Jesus, they're blessings.

◆　　　　　◆　　　　　◆

The great philosophic debate of the twentieth century has been about which economic system can best bring people material prosperity. It hasn't been about the intrinsic value of physical wealth, or its relationship to complex human needs. Liberal and conservative agree that financial success is just the thing to keep families together, to "afford" people a sense of redemption and self-worth, to allow them to co-exist in peaceful community with one another, to behave in a manner acceptable to their society. This is the goal of contemporary public policy on the left and the right. Liberal capitalism envisions the slow development of a prosperous world where every individual has the opportunity to work toward material success within the human marketplace. Socialism imagines the engineering of a physical paradise for all people, regardless of status or ability.

But we beg the question in framing our choice as one between capitalism and socialism, between the material gospels of self-interest and social welfare. This is no choice at all. Can either of these really provide us with what we most need? Both are finite and objective faiths, empty of moral imperative and spiritual meaning. Both treat human beings only as consumers and producers. Both teach that all values are material values, that even love and charity are acts of quantifiable value.

But what would happen if someone refused to define himself by his economic status? What if someone came along and insisted that there's nothing ultimately valuable in material progress? What if someone were to treat the getting and spending of money, neither with contempt, nor with respect, but with indifference? That would make him the world's first real revolutionary. Marx says man consists of the material he makes and is made by. What's revolutionary about that? People have always assumed such a thing without even thinking about it. That was our philosophy before there *was* philosophy. Jesus is the revolutionary. Karl Marx is one of the most conventional thinkers who ever lived.

The gospel is a rebuke of both liberal and conservative political theory, an offense to free-market and state-based economic systems, an indictment of the rapacity of the rich and the covetousness of the poor, all because it preaches a kind of wealth that we can't count or control or even very well understand. Wealth of the *spirit* is for Jesus the only treasure worth having, and he speaks rapturously of its abundance — "good measure, pressed down, shaken together, running over" — waiting for all who would accept it.

VII

BEYOND ME

*He who sees the infinite in all things, sees God. He
who sees the ratio only, sees himself only.*

"There is No Natural Religion" (second series)

THE CHRISTIAN CHURCH today is obsessed with its standing
in the world. Perhaps, as with all people, we find ourselves
drawn ineluctably into the universal struggle for political and
economic and social power. Maybe, of all people, we are
haunted by the past, when the One Holy Catholic and Apostolic
Church ruled over all the earth it cared to know about. That
kind of power and glory has certainly waned over the last few
centuries, and many believers see in its eclipse a terrible
theological dilemma. If Jesus spoke truly when he said that "I
have overcome the world," why has his church continued to
struggle, often unsuccessfully, against it? It looks more like "the
world" has overcome *us*.

The common wisdom is that western Christianity has been
slowly backed against the wall by "secularization," a process in
which traditional religious considerations in public and private
affairs give way to other, more immediate social, political, and
individual concerns. As a result of secularization, we are told,
the church finds itself caught more and more without proper
resources or direction, squeezed into an ever-tighter
marketplace, excluded increasingly from positions of power,
subject finally to ridicule from the media and the academy. In
recent years the relationship between "secular" and "sacred" has

become contentious and unpleasant. We are given to understand that the two are now engaged in a kind of "cultural warfare," but this is greatly overstated: the church has been able to manage only guerrilla tactics against the numberless heathen.

Secularization is a popular and widely accepted theory, but it's an odd one nonetheless, since the world is secular by definition (Latin, *saecula*). Is it really an insight to say that the world is slowly becoming, well, the world? It's no more the world now than it ever was, and its values have always been the same. Only the labels have changed.

But the theology of the Christian response to this alleged process is just as peculiar. And, once again, the difficulty is predicated on our *chronic refusal to distinguish between finite and infinite*. When our understandings are not rooted in this, Jesus' most crucial distinction, we find ourselves saying and believing some very foolish things.

Allow me one quick example. Perhaps you remember the campaign an American evangelist waged a few years back to protest the screening of "The Last Temptation of Christ." In this film he believed that the sacred was coming under attack by the secular, and he decided to do something about it. The evangelist used his organization's considerable resources to orchestrate a protest at various theaters, a letter-writing campaign, and a product boycott of the parent company. The film itself was generally acclaimed by critics, but received only limited screenings, and quickly disappeared. Then, a short time later, a small fire broke out in the studios of the film company responsible for "Last Temptation." It was nothing major, but some valuable props and film and other material were lost. And when the minister appeared on television the next day he was wearing the smuggest of expressions. He proudly proclaimed that God had been at work here. God had been angered, and he had struck back. A miracle.

The minister himself had performed a greater miracle than

that. How so? He had taken Elohim Adonai, the Lord God Almighty, Preserver of Israel, Lion of the Tribe of Judah, the King of Kings, the Horn of Salvation, the Sun of Righteousness, the Great *I Am* — and turned him into a petty arsonist. Not even a very good one.

How exactly is that a triumph? A truly infinite being, the God beyond all our petty and vindictive little gods, *willed into being* the material of that studio, the screenplay's author, the film's producer, its celluloid, the movie theaters in which it was shown and the eyes with which it was viewed. With own his hands created he them. All his bets are covered, so to speak. If there is such a being, all true power has always been his alone, from the beginning. But the minister was excited about a deity who sets off small electrical fires. That seems like an awfully wimpy sort of a god; I'd as soon do homage to Ra, or Baal, or some poor Druid's shrubbery.

When we worship finite gods we shouldn't be surprised that they manage to accomplish so little for us. And we aren't. On the contrary, in our quest to remain a prominent ideology of the world we're easily pleased by statistics showing a slight increase in nationwide church attendance, or by a legislative victory for "religious freedom," or by faulty wiring in secular film studios. It's true that we once hoped to cast mountains into the sea, but when we play by the world's rules we rightfully expect to assume the world's limitations.

Now an obsession with temporal power and its many tools is understandable in people for whom there's nothing of interest beyond those things presented by sense and knowledge, and no values that extend beyond the short scope of their lives. But followers of Jesus of Nazareth, transformed and inspired by his unique vision of the world, should be the first to see temporal authority and fame as mere spectacle. We of all people should know that lasting power can't be measured by the usual means, that infinite truth escapes all finite measures, and is wholly independent of human response to it. We should be unmoved by social movements, market strategies, or political ideologies, knowing that what Jesus calls "the kingdom of God" works on a different level entirely, unaffected by the machinations of the world, operating almost at a sub-atomic level, growing in spirit, working in community, acting in faith, an invisible kingdom without possibility of barrier or border. This hasn't been the case.

Christians treat human boundaries and distinctions, money and resources, social trends and political movements, as potential obstacles to people of faith. Without access to the current tools of secular power we imagine ourselves, and the gospel, to be ineffectual, powerless, or irrelevant. Many prominent ministers today argue that the failure of the church lies not in its abandonment of the gospel but in its inability to embrace a marketing orientation in a market-driven society. Money and political clout and a "high profile" are what is needed to effectively preach Jesus' message, they say; huge buildings and advertising campaigns and product boycotts are required to proclaim the gospel. We're told that our success can be charted by graphs and polls that sample the vagaries of human affection. Church attendance figures are often taken as valid measures of achievement, and the success of "Marches for Jesus" the true mark of God's power in the world.

What puny, fragile gods we adore! Recently I heard a sermon on evangelism in my home parish in which an elderly minister warned that we, the people of God, had better be careful. If we don't do our job the Christian message could pass away entirely, so that our children would be bereft of the Way and the Truth. It's up to us, he said, to preserve two millennia of Christ's work in the world. God is counting on us. Now this is an amazing, a staggering thing for a minister of a Christian church to say: that it's possible for the Truth to expire. If it can pass away, was it ever really true? Christians are not in the business of promoting an endangered practice, like Gaelic or duckpins. Infinite truth needs no preservation, and it requires no defense. Either we testify to that Truth, which stands on its own, to the end of time, or all our words amount to exactly nothing. If the "Christian message" dies then it was a finite message, and was always destined for failure and obliteration. If Jesus ends up in the dustbin of history, then that's where he always belonged.

This is the message preached by the Pharisee Gamaliel, the great rabbi and tutor to Saul of Tarsus. The book of Acts describes a meeting of the Sanhedrin, the high Jewish council, convened in Jerusalem to deal with the problems created by the infant Christian community. In that meeting Gamaliel stands before his colleagues and suggests a truly radical course of action: doing nothing at all. Let be, he says. Remember the rebel Theudas. Four hundred men once backed him, and where is his movement now? Remember that you once had grave concerns about Judas the Galilean. But he too is long gone. I want to suggest, he concludes, that you "keep away from these men and let them alone, for if this plan or undertaking is of men, it will fail; but if it is of God, you will not be able to overthrow them." Gamaliel was "held in high regard by the people" for the remarkable breadth of his vision. He understood something we may have forgotten — that, regardless of bumbling endeavor and chance event, in spite of all the money and legislation in the world, what is finite will pass away, and what is infinite will endure.

◆   ◆   ◆

Any kind of temporal power in the modern world is power derived from the state, but the state would gladly have some divine sanction to legitimate its use of power more fully. This is the only role the world still wants the Christian church to perform for it, and we're glad to be of use, seizing upon any opportunity, no matter how craven, to look relevant and important.

But we do the principalities even greater honor in those moments that we claim to hate and oppose them! Consider the activist minister I mentioned in the last chapter, who believes it's the church's job to petition government to create a more equitable social and economic system. His unquestioned assumption is that it lies within the power of government to realize our greatest values. The kingdoms apparently *can* "achieve on earth a perfection that is only to be found in the beyond." So it becomes the sacred task of Christians to petition the governments to get them to do that. The conclusion is clear: it's Caesar that matters. Caesar can make things right for us.

This is just as true of political activists on the religious right, for whom "morality" takes the place of "justice" as the supposedly infinite value. They believe without question that what Caesar does is all-important — it simply never occurs to them to question, as Jesus does, this age-old assumption. The debate on school prayer provides a perfect example. The right knows that its values are at stake when government considers the use of prayer in public school. For them, prayer has a specific civic purpose that will be lost if neglected. But in the gospels Jesus seems not to care about its civic function. He describes prayer as an intimate, discreet, deeply personal act. He notes that public prayer is often an empty formality, meant for the ears of others rather than for God. Probably for this reason he usually prays alone, and recommends that others find a quiet place to pray in secret to "the Father": "The Father, who sees in secret, will reward you." No law is needed to establish that kind of prayer, and no law can prevent it.

Both the left and the right want to assert their own gospels in the political power game. Both "judge according to the flesh," to use Jesus' expression. Both render unto Caesar the things that are God's, since Caesar is all they really care about. It doesn't appear to bother them that much of the time they're fighting each other, two sides of a single coin minted by Caesar and bearing his likeness. Maybe it's too difficult for us to believe that what Caesar does is ultimately unimportant. Caesar is the focus of so much of our lives, our Savior and our Satan, our brightest hope and darkest fear. There are few things we love so much as our country's constitution, and nothing we hate so much as the men and women who enact it. Almost everything good and bad in our lives we attribute in some way to "the powers that be" and the ideas behind them.

Jesus calls into question this universal human obsession. First of all, he maintains that the powers and principalities are not in God's hands at all, but in the hands of Satan, the Adversary, whom he calls "the ruler of this world." That certainly would explain why he wants no part of the kingdoms we Christians strive so ceaselessly to control! Secondly, Jesus warns that no one can serve two masters: "You will either love the first and hate the second, or hate the first and love the second." One master will always win out. If we live in the world, then the world, where our "rulers lord it over [us], and [our] great men make their authority felt," is likely to prevail. So Jesus is anxious that his followers make the conscious choice to abandon the kingdoms of earth and all their machinations, and live in the eternal kingdom of heaven, where "the one who rules is like the one who serves."

Finally, and most importantly, Jesus believes that the kingdoms of the earth are *finite*, and therefore of no lasting consequence. For this reason he steadfastly refuses to try to control them. "Human glory means nothing to me," he insists. Jesus responds to all forms of temporal power with absolute indifference. He devotes little thought or energy to the powers that be, never questioning Roman law, picking no fights with the prevailing economic and political institutions. For Jesus, hating temporal power in a sense is just like loving it — both reactions afford it more attention than it deserves. He pays no attention to the Caesar of the day. Caesar eventually dies and is replaced by another Caesar anyway. But that shouldn't be surprising: "*Every* plant which my heavenly Father has not planted will be pulled up by the roots."

Of course, Jesus of Nazareth does lay claim to great power, to the greatest power there is, including power over life and death. This is what humanity has always dreamed of, and many, beginning with Adam and Eve, have tried to attain. Jesus' method is only one of many. But his is dramatically different from that of others, from all that have come before and since. His is the paradoxical method of *relinquishing* all power — as well as wealth, prestige, and life. He insists that true life cannot declare itself except through this surrender. According to Jesus, power and life can't be seized by storm, siege, or subterfuge. They aren't taken, as you might steal fruit from a tree, but can only be accepted, as you might accept a cup of bitter wine.

Read the gospels and you'll find that Jesus' idea of power, and his uses of it, are as unlike the world's, and the church's, as they can be. These are crucial differences, and illustrative ones. They play out most poignantly in his three major moments of temptation, each of which harkens back to the first one in Eden. Consider: a man in a Garden (Gethsemane) feels tempted to oppose the Infinite will. His decision, like that of Adam and Eve, is a matter of life and death, and predicated on the need to be like God, to obtain heretofore unimaginable power. But Jesus doesn't *want* to eat the fruit (or drink the wine, in this case — after so many generations the fruit of our disobedience has apparently fermented). He says he'd rather let that cup pass from his lips. Maybe he's thinking about the agony of crucifixion, or questioning the value of his death, wondering whether the men sleeping peacefully nearby are worth the effort. His strange garden soliloquy, however, leads this new Adam to a new decision: "Not my will, but yours." This is the only statement of faith there is — the bowing of the finite to the infinite, the giving up of the technologies and religions of control, the denial of self in the face of a will and purpose that transcend it.

There's an even more telling temptation than that. I'm thinking of Jesus' encounter with the "Adversary" in the Judean wilderness. He has been fasting for forty days when Satan appears and tells him that all power over the earth can be his if he simply defers to its source. (Satan himself points out what Jesus already knows — that *he* is the real distributor of this world's power: "It has been handed over to me to give to anyone I choose.") The proposition is a simple one. And here, unlike in Eden, the Adversary attempts no tricks! Rather than assume the guise of a smooth-talking reptile, he appears as himself and quite honestly points out to Jesus that the whole world is his for the asking. The three prospects — freedom from harm, bread for the masses, and all earth's kingdoms — are enticing, but Jesus rejects each in succession. You'd have to be ignorant to feel content with bread alone, selfish to want to control all the kingdoms of the earth, faithless to test the source of your salvation. And what would it profit him to gain a mortal world and to lose his immortal soul?

Jesus' final refusal of temporal power in Jerusalem leads him to Golgotha and the cross. Offense leads to offense in the gospels, and the cross is the last and greatest of them all, the heart of their scandal. An omnipotent God chooses to reject building, bread, and sword, to express himself in powerlessness and shame rather than in economic and political might? It's too much to fathom, even at a distance of two millennia: that *real* power in the world looks like weakness, that God embraces the fragile and feeble things of this world to shame the strong. Jesus takes the cross, not to defeat his enemies, but to subject himself to them completely, to act out in his final parable the truth that to become the greatest in the kingdom of heaven you have to be the least in the kingdom of earth. For three hours he is just that.

Peter vehemently opposes Jesus here, and he acts as the instrument of Jesus' third temptation. When he tells Peter that the Son of Man, as servant rather than master of all, must undergo suffering and death, Peter stridently objects. Surely that's not the way to power and life! But Jesus has already heard this spiel in the wilderness, and he knows its source. He calls Peter "Satan," and then explains why: "For you are not on the side of God, but of men." Peter says nothing in return, no doubt offended by the harshness of Jesus' rebuke and by the very idea that to be on the side of Satan is to be on the side "of men."

The church that Peter led had a terrible time trying to explain Jesus' crucifixion to potential converts. As Paul notes, based on his own experience with preaching the gospel, the crucifixion is "a scandal to Jews and foolishness to Gentiles." The most common method of avoiding this scandal has been to treat the cross as a trick, a kind of magical feat by which Jesus cleverly eludes his enemies, and later appears again to defeat them. So, rather than a renunciation of power, the cross then becomes an oblique way of *gaining* earthly power. Rome, unfazed by the spectacular irony, eventually adopted the cross as a battle standard against the heathen hordes of the north! In this way the symbol of submission became once again a symbol of domination, the universal culture of human violence regained its ancient legitimacy, and we were able to return to our traditional understandings about how real power is used by God, and by people. Those understandings prevail to this day.

I once spent an unhappy year working for a wire service in Columbus, Ohio. During that time I met and befriended an unusual young man named Andrew. Andrew was a kind of religious bohemian — part skeptic, part mystic, and part devout Catholic. He was struggling at that time with the idea of entering the priesthood. The prospect was both alluring and appalling to him, and weighed all the more heavily because of his parents' expectations. Andrew's father was a steelworker, a deeply religious man who rose early every morning to make Mass before his shift began. He hadn't missed a weekday Mass in six years. His mother attended far fewer services than her husband, but made up for it with her daily devotions. Every room in their home was fitted out with various icons, candles, and crucifixes. There were four statuettes of the Virgin Mary. Andy joked that his mother showed a marked preference for Mary over her son.

His parents drove out from Pittsburgh to visit him one weekend. They had planned an outing, about an hour's trip, to see a great iron crucifix that someone had erected in the Midwestern countryside. People from all over went to see the thing, stuck in the middle of cornfields. I joined them out of curiosity, and during the trip finally got to know Andy's father, a man I had heard much about, and had admired long before I met. He was tall, a little shy, with dark, intense eyes like those of his son. He loved Andy, believed that he was destined to be a great priest, and saw him as his own greatest accomplishment in life, the fruit of his devotion to the gospel. I remember feeling a little awed by the strong and simple faith of this quiet steelworker, and thinking that the Catholic church could probably use more men like him.

After a longish drive and dozens of Midwestern turns (each exactly 90 degrees) we found the iron crucifix. It wasn't huge, but it was an affecting piece of twisted metal, graphic and gothically sinister. The figure of Jesus seemed to be half-yelling, half-crying. The body was all bones, unnaturally contorted on the iron rack. It was obvious that Andy's father was deeply affected by what he saw. He watched silently, but his hands worked in his pockets, and a look of pain or dolor sometimes winced across his face. I waited to hear what, if anything, this gentle pilgrim would say about the mystery of the cross. And after a while he did speak. "Such a death," he said. "*Somebody's going to pay for that.*"

Jesus' rebuke of his disciples should ring freshly in our ears: "Do you still not understand?"

♦   ♦   ♦

Recently we seem to have grown cynical about the possibility of growth and positive change by way of political legislation and military might. After many thousands of years Caesar looks a little tired, and more and more of us are beginning to leave the ramparts and go tend our gardens, to try to bring about personal rather than social redemption. This is a welcome development. But even this doesn't prompt us to abandon our favorite values — we're too wily in our ways for that. Instead we redirect them, re-assert them on a more intimate level. The quest for power continues under the title of "self-empowerment," and it's evidently a quest with great attractions.

Consider the growing number of ministers today who preach the popular philosophy of the "human potential" movement: that God wants people to be happy, wealthy, empowered, and long-lived, and that all of this can be achieved if they discard the habits of negative thinking. By means of a more positive and self-confident attitude people can *will* themselves to a more satisfying and fulfilling life, and this is their greatest goal. Christianity, it is argued, should reform itself to enable people in their quest for self-actualization. Forget the morbid emphasis on sin and repentance. Lent, for instance, that miserable and dreary time. Lent should stand for Let's Eliminate Negative Thinking. After all, you can't achieve prosperity and empowerment when you're wearing sackcloth and ashes!

The first question to ask about a message preached by a Christian minister in a Christian church is whether it's the gospel of Christ. Preachers of the "human potential" movement testify to some other gospel, a gospel according to them, and they should acknowledge as much. In Matthew, Mark, Luke, and John, Jesus is sometimes a very *un*happy man. And he does little for himself. Instead he teaches his followers that their lives should be dedicated to the service of *others*. He argues that the soul grows by subtraction. He points toward self-emptying rather than self-fulfillment as the first step of discipleship: "If any want to become my followers let them *deny themselves* and take up the cross." Throughout his ministry Jesus offers warnings to the self-satisfied, the "self-made," the self-important. It takes a willful blindness to avoid seeing that in the gospels.

Self-fulfillment means being full of yourself. Jesus offers in its place the experience of *ecstasy*. We need to join ourselves to something that completely transcends our mood or job or backache or bank account of the day, something that gets us outside of ourselves altogether. He points toward this as the only way we can relieve ourselves of the enormous burden of self that is the source, rather than the solution, to our problems. That's what "ecstasy" means — literally, "standing outside" of yourself. (Jesus lives in this state, though his family takes it for insanity: "He is *beside* himself.") It is a chance to unlock the iron doors of selfhood and see more than what little is evident in peering through what Blake calls "the narrow chinks" of our personal caverns. It's an experience of liberation that reveals our quests for "fulfillment" or "empowerment" as lonely and hollow. Jesus' life, ending on an implement of execution, doesn't fit our idea of personal fulfillment, but it gave way to the experience of ecstasy.

Today it is held as the highest moral endeavor to pay close and constant attention to your immediate physical and emotional needs. These needs have now taken on the aspect of sacred objects; devotion to them is believed to provide us a kind of salvation. Selfishness is preached as the truest and noblest expression of self, and individual empowerment its proper profession. No other value, not even love, is considered worthy of our commitment unless it can satisfy those fundamental requirements. Loving others is great, we're told, but first you have to concentrate on loving yourself. "I am the greatest thing that will ever happen to me!" is the new mantra, and a "self-fulfilling" prophecy if ever there was one.

What Jesus teaches is what it takes a good rolfer about ten

years to discover: that we're not able to effect our own salvation. Our wills are finite and deficient. We can't even properly *ask* for what we need, much less obtain it. Yet we go on constructing our personal towers to heaven, "look[ing] to one another for approval," fashioning gods in our image, living in the same dull round, staring at our emotional navels. But like Adam and Eve, like Icarus, like Alexander and Napoleon, like our father and spouse and best friend, like every Possibility Thinker and every Primal Screamer, we always come up against the limits of our finitude, even as we deny that there are any limits to what we can do or be, even as we go each to a cold grave, our potential finally impotent.

The work of self-love and self-empowerment is evanescent and infertile. It's inevitably frantic and self-defeating. But still, in this vacuum created by the absence of the gospels, we can't seem to think of anything else to do with ourselves. The pursuit of selfish goals continues to mark the rhythm of modern life, and its litany of boredom and frustration can be heard on every street: "I tried aerobics. I tried est. I tried shopping. I tried sex." Every declaration is the same. I tried me. I tried me. I tried me. I tried me. But I never tried *you*.

VIII

WHAT SHALL I DO?

The Moral Virtues in their Pride
Did o'er the World triumphant ride
In Wars & Sacrifice for Sin,
And Souls to Hell ran trooping in.
The Accuser, Holy God of All
This Pharisaic Worldly Ball,
Amidst them in his Glory Beams
Upon the Rivers & the Streams.
Then Jesus rose & said to Me,
"Thy Sins are all forgiven thee."
Loud Pilate Howl'd, loud Caiphas yell'd,
When they the Gospel Light beheld.
It was when Jesus said to Me,
"Thy sins are all forgiven thee."

"The Everlasting Gospel"

WE MAY eventually abandon our pursuit of money and power, of all self-centered and short-sighted goals. We may even learn from our disillusionment in the products and leaders and ideologies that promise us much more than they can deliver. It could be that we're actually better off for having tried them and given them up — even if Sisyphus was frustrated, he was in fabulous shape. But in our quest for enduring values the question remains: what *will* last? What *is* worthy of my faith and devotion? Where can I look for true hope and final salvation? And what shall I do to attain it?

For the Jews the answer is obvious. Salvation has only one form. It came first to the chosen people of God, as a gift, a great gift from on high, handed to Moses on Mount Sinai. It is the Law. Only the Law can straddle the gap between finite and infinite, provide intercourse between the mountain and the desert, offer refuge from suffering and injustice and maybe even death. The prospect of God's eternal fairness and rectitude has always provided the Jews with their greatest hope and consolation. Fear not, for God is just. The law is our salvation.

The Jews are not alone in this belief. It's the practice of many peoples to address and define their world through the logic and structure of law. Most of the advances of human civilization we attribute to its broad powers. It is law that supports the moral and judicial systems, the economic organization, the whole social contract on which communal life is based. Law sets the boundaries, establishes the hierarchies, maintains the discriminations that give sense and order to the movements of human life. Law even provides the logical structures that make technical and moral progress possible. We understand all physical events in the universe by means of law — specifically, the law of cause and effect. This is the founding precept of scientific understanding: something happens because something makes it happen. But we apply it with equal confidence to the moral realm, where again one action requires another. "An eye for an eye" has all the reasonableness and beautiful congruity of Newton's laws of motion, and this has long been held as a basic ethical tenet, dating back to the Hebrews, Babylonians, and other ancient peoples. With scientific law we impute a comfortable consistency to all physical events. With sacred law we honor specific rules of conduct that serve as reassuring markers in our difficult moral landscape. With secular law we enjoy personal protection against much of the unfairness and injustice of social and natural life. Now these great bodies of legal doctrine don't always do for us what we think they should, but we can't seem to do without them.

And only one man objects; perhaps you have guessed who.

Jesus of Nazareth asks some unique questions about the assumptions and motives behind our devotion to law. To begin with, he teaches and demonstrates that cause doesn't necessarily match effect, either in the material or the moral realm. In healing a lame beggar, calming the sea with a word, or feeding thousands with a few loaves and fish, Jesus presents us with physical occurrences in the world that have no *material* cause — an intolerable prospect for beings devoted to knowledge, order, and sense. Further, and again by means of example, he argues that events in the world may have no *moral* cause. For Jesus, there's no question of people getting their "just deserts" on earth. He claims that "God is kind to the ungrateful and selfish," that the Father "causes the sun to rise on the bad as well as the good, and sends down rain to fall on the upright and the wicked alike." He objects to the common belief that illness or misfortune is a punishment for sin, either ours or our parents'. To an assembled group he recalls a recent tragedy to illustrate his point: "The Tower of Siloam fell on eighteen men and killed them. Do you think that these men were worse than anyone else living in Jerusalem?" Of course not — and herein lies our problem. It can be desperately frustrating to live in a world that doesn't conform to our expectations of it, a world in which random occurrences and "acts of God" don't fit our understanding of what is *just*. And yet Jesus wants to deny his listeners their habit of imposing on events in a free universe a meaning they can tolerate.

Jesus challenges all the human delusions of control that law serves to prompt. He argues that our wills and actions don't necessarily bring about their intended effects. You simply can't *make* things in your life turn out the way you want, try as you may. And neither can you change other people. They are free; as the disciples discovered, you can't determine who they'll be or what they'll do. You can't make someone reconcile with you, says Jesus. But that doesn't mean you shouldn't try anyway. You have to forgive your neighbor even if he doesn't accept your forgiveness, even if you think he'll probably wrong you again. In an undetermined universe you can never know what consequences your actions will bring. So you need to act based on considerations other than those of consequence.

Jesus apparently believes that law encourages people to care about nothing *but* consequence and outward results. The effect of this is the spiritual atrophy he sees everywhere. So he harshly condemns, even vilifies the law's protectors and interpreters; the Sadducees and Pharisees and priests and lawyers are often portrayed by him as evil people. These are the most prominent citizens of Judea, men who don't lie or murder or steal or commit adultery, who observe even the smallest rituals and prohibitions of daily Jewish life as sacred law and tradition dictate. There are no legal scholars more finely trained than the Pharisees. But Jesus calls them "blind guides," "hypocrites," and "children of hell."

How could this be true of men so fully devoted and obedient to the law? Because law is *external*. Law allows people to concern themselves with outward behavior, with events evident to the senses, with all apparent consequence. In this way they can ignore the unseen impulse for their behavior, the measure of what they really are. This is the basis for all of Jesus' accusations of the Pharisees: "You clean the outside of cup and dish, while the inside is full of what you have gotten by violence and selfishness." By contrast Jesus emphasizes the inner impulse for behavior. "Clean the inside of cup and dish first," he says, and provides specific examples of what he means. There's no point in giving gifts at the altar as expiation if you're not inwardly at peace with your neighbor. Fasting doesn't do any good if there is no real penitence behind it. If you have sex with someone in your mind, it's a reality in your heart. Blake:

> *A truth that's told with bad intent*
> *Beats all the lies you can invent.*

The Pharisees' "bad intent" is to take advantage of the external nature of the law, to bend it toward their selfish purposes. They believe that outward observance of the law will justify them before God. They already know it justifies them before others. The Pharisees are good, decent, law-abiding citizens whose behavior convinces others of their worthiness, thereby affording them social power and prestige.

Jesus takes note of this strategy — "You are those who justify yourselves before others" — and doesn't deny that it works quite well. But he does deny that devotion to the law will justify the Pharisees before God. *All* finite beings are imperfect, he argues, and therefore are condemned under the law before God: "Did not Moses give you the law? Yet not one of you keeps the law." And yet, in spite of this, the Pharisees continue to place their greatest hopes on the very instrument of their damnation! They look at the debt and see only the payment. Jesus is stunned by this irony: "It is Moses who accuses you, the very Moses on whom you set your hope!" In fact, they are all the more deeply condemned by the law because of their devotion to it, like a soldier hoist by his own petard. Worse still (and this is what makes Jesus so livid), they drag many others down with them: "You shut up the kingdom of heaven in people's faces."

Jesus remarks often on the paradoxical rewards for the Pharisees' pious legalism. "If you were blind you would have no guilt," he explains. "But now that you say 'We see', your guilt remains." By contrast, he advises his followers to avoid legal and moral judgment altogether, to break the cycle of sin and condemnation and guilt that is the source rather than the solution to their problems. Otherwise, he warns them, "the standard you use will be used for you."

Ultimately, law does not justify, but condemn. It condemns all of its subjects as it first condemned Adam and Eve. It makes transgressors of free beings, and then requires their punishment. Adam and Eve live in perfection until Yahweh introduces a law. (In a garden, the first law is bound to be horticultural.) The result is lightning-quick: sin and death. Yahweh later presents more sacred law — to Moses up on Mount Sinai. That great gift was meant to bind the finite and the infinite in an eternal covenant, but it served only and immediately to separate Yahweh further from his children. The law was written on brittle stone, and it shattered at Moses' feet even before he could read it aloud. The Ten were expanded into 613 separate commandments, and the chosen people broke every last one. Maybe it's this woeful record that prompts Jesus to claim, quite offensively, that salvation is "impossible" for men and women. And yet the law remains, he insists, impermeable and merciless. He should know; it requires his death too. His former supporters shout it up to Pilate: "We have a law, and by that law he ought to die." Jesus goes without argument.

◆   ◆   ◆

> *Behold, the days are coming, says the Lord, when I will make a new covenant with the house of Judah, not like the covenant which I made with their fathers when I took them by the hand to bring them out of the land of Egypt, my covenant which they broke, though I was their husband, says the Lord. But this is the covenant which I will make with the house of Israel after those days, says the Lord: I will put my law within them, and I will write it upon their hearts; and I will be their God, and they shall be my people. And no longer shall each man teach his neighbor and each his brother, saying, 'Know the Lord,' for they shall all know me, from the least of them to the greatest, says the Lord; for I will forgive their iniquity, and I will remember their sin no more.*

This is a kind of prose poem. It's a strange piece of work, both ecstatic and restrained, mystical in concept but lucid in its vision. Jeremiah speaks with the voice of prophecy: one day Yahweh will give to his people a new covenant. It will replace the one they couldn't keep. This covenant will be based on forgiveness rather than judgment. And Yahweh will put it within his people, "write it upon their hearts" rather than cold hard stone, so that people will come to *know* God. The impossible will happen, says Jeremiah — the infinite will be known by finite beings.

Of course, all of this is blasphemy to Jews, and plain silliness to Greeks, envisioned by a man who sometimes covered himself in manure before he went out preaching. But there it is. It even happened many hundreds of years after the death of Jeremiah that members of a Jewish sect began to teach that this new covenant had in fact been established. Its founder was a rural Galilean, a man who was also God. And this God-Man had died — been crucified, in fact. But through him the powers of the infinite have become available to all human beings, mediated by a new law and a new way of being.

Back to the text. Here again the gospel stories weave into one another, each highlighting different aspects of this, the most crucial question of all. In Matthew a Pharisee asks Jesus which is "the greatest commandment of the Law." In Mark a scribe challenges him to identify the "first" commandment. In Luke a lawyer asks what he must do to gain eternal life. In these last two stories it's worth noting that those who speak with Jesus seem like intelligent men who really are interested in the answer for its own sake, though Luke doesn't like the lawyer anyway. The lawyer actually doesn't ask Jesus a legal question; it's more of a personal one. He wants to know what he must do to inherit eternal life. As is his habit, Jesus turns the question back on his interlocutor: "How do you read it?" The lawyer has an answer. Love God with all your heart and soul and strength, and love your neighbor as yourself. He speaks as if he knew it all by heart, and Jesus praises him for his response — his answer in Matthew is the same. (Note that two commandments are provided, though the asker specifies one only.)

The lawyer then moves to cross-examine. "And who is my neighbor?" he asks. Luke suggests that the lawyer asks this to "justify himself," but it's hard to say how his question does that. It reads like a natural follow-up, since the law does concern itself with what status qualifies one to be a neighbor. Only fellow Jews are included, for instance, but what are the other criteria? Now would seem to be the time for Jesus to hand down a shrewd ruling of law, a clever exegesis of sacred legal precepts, a closely reasoned discourse about who qualifies for this very rare and special treatment. Instead he tells a story.

Jesus wants to focus on the lawyer's original question: "What shall I do?" Rather than status, he is interested in what *deeds* qualify as an expression of neighborliness and love. After all, it's by their "fruits" that people are best known. So Jesus draws the lawyer away from the abstract religious and legal angles and presents to him a specific human situation. He tells of a Jew, traveling the dangerous road to Jericho, who is attacked by robbers, stripped and beaten, left "half dead" on the roadside, even ignored by other Jews who pass his way. Finally he's approached by a natural enemy. But rather than add to his miseries, this man soothes his wounds with oil and wine, binds them, puts him on his own animal, gets him into a room, even pays the innkeeper in advance to look after him. The parable, as do most of Jesus' parables, consists of descriptions of actions — what the Samaritan *did*.

Once again Jesus takes the usual approach and skews it. The lawyer appears to be thinking of the "neighbor" as a type of person deserving very special treatment. He wants to know to whom he must afford such a distinction. It would be shocking enough for Jesus to insist that Jews must treat Samaritans as neighbors. But the news is even worse than that. In the story it's the *Jew* who is beaten and bloody and the *Samaritan* who performs the life-saving service. The lawyer, a Jew, could never equate himself with a Samaritan — in this story he can see himself only as the Jew. He travels occasionally, and has surely worried about thieves, especially on roads like the mountainous one to Jericho. So in this parable he can't see himself as neighbor but as *victim*. The neighbor isn't the one in need, but one who comes to his aid.

The angle of Jesus' argument is painfully acute. You may see yourself as a good neighbor, he implies, dispensing gracious favors to friends and relations. In truth you are a wretch, a slowly dying man, and in desperate need of the mercy of all, even of your greatest enemy. The lawyer considers any Samaritan an inferior life form. He carefully avoids even speaking the word "Samaritan"; he would certainly abhor being touched by one. The man needs to be *beaten senseless* before he can see a new and entirely different sense. He needs to lose his every defense before he can become susceptible to the act of love, the only act that can save his stagnant and selfish life.

What kind of a "law" takes the form of a story? What kind of a law could establish a covenant that actually works? What must its characteristics be? First, it has to bridge the gap between the finite and the infinite. The "Love Commandment" does that. This single commandment is made up of two parts that treat the love of God and the love of people as the same action and event. Through this new covenant, embodied in Jesus, the Infinite assumes a finite form, and takes up residence in the human heart. How better, then, to love God than by loving others? Burnt offerings don't suffice. "Learn what it means," advises Jesus: "'I desire mercy and not sacrifice'." The priest and Levite believed they loved God even as they passed the bleeding man by. They were wrong.

Secondly, an infinite law has to be free from the illusions of cause and effect. Real love can't be conditional, predicated upon someone's contrition or reformation. It doesn't require a response of any kind. Neither is it guaranteed to end our dislike of one another, or settle our quarrels, or provide a happy ending. People are to love one another without just cause, and regardless of effect. For Jesus, love is always cut loose, there for its own sake and no other. There is no word about whether the Samaritan was rewarded for his kindness — or whether the Jew lived through the night.

Thirdly, such a law has to be enabling rather than disabling. It should open up possibilities instead of limit them, tell us what we *can* do rather than what we can't. This is exactly what Jesus does again and again, most notably in his "sermon on the mount." The law Moses delivered from his mountain consisted mostly of "thou shalt nots." With the Love Commandment Jesus takes the negatives of the old law and replaces them with the potential and possibility he sees in all life. Augustine paraphrased it to good effect: "Love, and do as you please." Love enables Jesus to do many things, even things traditionally seen as sinful. His devotion to love leads him to violate the Sabbath restrictions, to sit at table with Gentiles, to refuse submission to his parents, to turn away the law from a woman caught in adultery. And he enables others to act in love. He says human beings are free to eat what they want, to speak and live with whom they choose. They are masters of the Sabbath. They can forgive sins. They are free to love whenever, however, whomever they can. It's what the Samaritan does, not what he doesn't do, that comprises the true expression of love.

Finally, such a law has to point inward: it must be an internal rather than external standard. How should I act? How should I treat those around me? Well, how would I like to be treated? Look within yourself, Jesus suggests, and nowhere else. The Love Commandment thrusts us into a moral universe in which *we* have to make the determinations of what to do, how to act. No one else, not even God, will do that for us. (Jesus often refuses to do so for the disciples: "Why don't you judge for yourselves what is right?") There are no prescriptions provided to us by the Love Commandment, because it's not a traditional standard of law. In fact, it's not really "law" at all, but a way, a sign, a method of relation. Jesus points out what should have been obvious to us from the beginning — that a moral code can make sense only within the context of our relation to one another. He tells people to act in accordance with the central human dynamic composed of Self and Other, I and Thou. Treat others based on how you want to be treated. Love others as much as you love yourself.

This may sound fair and reasonable to us; we've heard it so many times now that it barely registers. But it implies a great many new things. As Jesus notes, "Every teacher of the law who has been instructed about the kingdom of heaven is like the owner of a house who brings out of his storeroom new treasures as well as old." And some of these new treasures are deeply offensive ones. For example, under the Love Commandment, the ways we decide to act may be *different.* My expression of love may not be yours, just as I may not want to be "done unto" the same way you want to be "done unto." "Love" cannot be defined and prescribed any more than "God" can (the root word of "definition" is "finite"). So responses made in love are relative to the heart and nature of every woman and man.

This is exactly what much of the Christian church has breathlessly opposed for ages. Each individual deciding for herself or himself how to live? We can't allow that. People will begin to do anything. *Everything* will be possible. But this is exactly Jesus' promise! "Nothing will be impossible for you," he tells his followers. And what else can infinity mean except the innumerable possibilities of a limitless universe? With this commandment Jesus announces the presence of a new world of wondrous freedom and responsibility where all our timid and lying moralities can find no place.

As finite beings we will by nature be confused, angered, and frightened by an infinite law. In the presence of the Love Commandment we have acted like the frightened Israelites in the Sinai who wanted to return to a secure life of slavery back in Egypt. We continue to prefer the original ten, since they work as an assurance that we're justified before God and man. Without them our whole moral groundwork would be rooted up. Our carefully structured controls, the consistency of our tastes, the censure of law, the mechanics of our wishes, the arbitrary boundaries between the possible and the permissible — all would evaporate like fog. Without the old law we would find ourselves placed in the Eternal Now, that staggering juncture of possibility where we're confronted with the freedom and responsibility of selfhood actualized in every moment.

The prospect is certainly a daunting one, but Jesus sees in it the proper task of humanity. He actually believes we're capable of living as autonomous beings, and offers many words of encouragement for facing whatever problems lie ahead: "Be of good cheer. I have overcome the world." And his new "law" does indeed enable us to act as moral agents, even in this century of terrifying indeterminacies. In fact, it challenges us to move from the two-dimensional world of the old law into the three-dimensional world we actually inhabit. Under the "Ten Commandments" you stand either within the law or without the law, inside or outside that line, a saint or a sinner (an arrangement the Pharisees loved). But in a three-dimensional universe lines are unimportant. There is no "side" to stand on. Infinity stretches before me, and I have to make terribly difficult decisions, even do things I'm not sure are right. For example, I may feel compelled by the Love Commandment to "bear false witness." There are situations — protecting a battered wife from her abusive husband, for instance — in which I may feel that I actually *need* to lie. Not that it's good to lie, but that it would be far worse in that situation to tell the truth. (In such predicaments Jesus advises his followers to be "wise as serpents" as well as "harmless as doves.") We can all think of hundreds of moral situations in which our choice is simply not between right and wrong. In fact it almost never is. We can feel trapped by these situations, entangled in ethical dilemmas from which there appears to be no escape. Jesus is himself presented with many such dilemmas. But in the gospels we see time after time how his commitment to love frees him to act.

The "Ten Commandments" can help us navigate our solitary way through the murky channels of the world. We certainly don't make ourselves free by breaking them, or any law. But in the realm of the infinite the old law has been supplanted for good, and a new one now obtains. Jesus makes this as clear as he can, reciting precept after precept of the old law and contradicting each boldly. "You have heard it said 'An eye for an eye and a tooth for a tooth.' But I tell you: offer no resistance to the wicked." "You have heard it said, 'Love your neighbor and hate your enemy.' But I tell you: love your enemies." Yes, Jesus, we have heard it was said. We have heard it was said by *Yahweh himself.* And now you say this. Can we continue to act like you didn't? Blake:

> *Jehovah's fingers Wrote the Law:*
> *Then Wept! Then rose in Zeal & Awe,*
> *And in the midst of Sinai's heat*
> *Hid it beneath his Mercy Seat.*
> *O Christians, Christians! tell me Why*
> *You rear it on your Altars high?*

Love is Jesus' only commandment. Love is the only verb he links to the Infinite. And, though it is still "a mortal danger" to beings composed of both, it has joined the finite to the infinite forever. "Up to the time of John it was the Law and the Prophets; from then onwards the kingdom of God has been preached, and everyone is forcing their way into it."

♦   ♦   ♦

What shall I do? This is the question we've been asking since Adam and Eve first gained free will. Jesus of Nazareth answers it. His answer is intelligible and urgent and always before us. "A new commandment I give you: love one another." Jesus addresses the most important moral question there is, and this is his answer. He calls his followers to something more real than self-fulfillment, more valuable than money, deeper than study and piety, greater than healing and tongues-speaking. He proffers a Law of Love, a basis for a new way of living. It's his single unifying teaching, his promised salvation, the filling full of our hollow law, the sum of all he has to say. Jesus calls his followers, first and foremost, to love others, to live for others. His own life he lives not for his benefit, but for the benefit of others, and he instructs his disciples to follow this example: "Love others, as I have loved you." Not to make yourself happy, or even to make yourself holy, but to empty yourself in service, to share your bread with the hungry and bring the homeless poor into your house, when you see the naked to cover him, and not hide yourself from your own flesh. To take away from the midst of you the yoke, the pointing of the finger, and speaking wickedness. To "do good to those who hate you, bless those who curse you, and pray for those who treat you badly."

What would happen if we used Jesus' criterion for discipleship rather than our own? What if we appraised ourselves solely in terms of the Love Commandment? Perhaps it would finally dawn on us that our categories of Catholic and Protestant and agnostic and humanist are finite and Pharisaic, that Jesus' real teachings are something other than we thought, something much more basic than our own, whose truth is revealed in the story of his life, and of ours. Maybe also we could finally see how every day his words are preached and lived in ways to which we've been completely oblivious. There are people of all sorts and conditions who try to love others as they love themselves. Quiet volunteers give of themselves unconditionally, working and ministering in hospitals, jails, and shelters. Poets call us to repentance from our lives of present ease and gratification. Musicians of every persuasion ecstatically proclaim the redemptive message of the gospel in their work. Doctors heal with compassion. Judges craft mercy from justice. Strangers offer selfless words of support; children help each other up when they fall. Each day people of every kind and description lose their lives a little to find them, and Christ's work of redemption is accomplished through them. But if they don't attend a church, or mouth a given religious and political dogma, much of which bears *no* relation to the teachings of Jesus, we don't count them among his followers. This can only hinder them from discovering the gospels, the crucial context for all selfless action. We build a church with doctrinal walls which, like the old law, you must stand either within or without. What did Peter say when he saw Jesus, transfigured, standing with Moses and Elijah? He suggested that they put up some buildings. That's what we have done, and we consider the larger ones the greatest accomplishments of Christendom. Maybe they are. But Jesus promises only to tear down the Temple, and raise in its place a body.

Who is that new Temple? Who follows this new law? Jesus doesn't define them by the houses in which they worship, or their adherence to doctrine, or their manner of dress or decorum. These are finite. In fact, remarkably, he doesn't even say it's those who proclaim his name: "It is not those who say to me 'Lord, Lord' who enter the kingdom of heaven, but the one who does the will of my father." He has only one standard — it's by their unconditional love that they'll be known. "Everyone will know you are my disciples if you have love for one another." He calls "mother and brothers" all those who hear his word and act on it. All others are Pharisees, who "do not practice what they preach." Remember the parable of the two sons, one who dutifully promised to work for his father in the vineyard, and didn't, and the other who refused, and then went out and worked anyway. With which son was that father pleased?

His entire ministry Jesus remains frustrated and amazed by the posturing of those who claim to be his followers. "Why do you keep calling me 'Lord, Lord,'" he complains, "and never do what I tell you?" Perhaps because the work of lips is easier than the work of hands and heart. But hearing and proclaiming the word, even the Infinite Word, is not enough. Jesus compares anyone who does that to "a stupid man who built his house on sand." Such a house can't possibly stand: "What a fall it had!"

AFTERWORD

What a fall we have had. For a long time our religion was the dominant force on the face of this green globe, the emblem and executor of all earth's power and glory. It must have seemed to Christians for well over a millennium that the kingdom of heaven was being established here among us, with the descendants of Peter as its rightful heirs. Our far-reaching control over the temporal realm we always took as a sign of the ultimate validity of our faith, and the durability of our religious institutions a sign of heaven's perpetual support.

And yet, as we waited and waited for the Christ to return, something peculiar happened: Christianity slowly devolved into only one of many available philosophies and practices, all competing for adherents in the ever-crowded marketplace of ideology and belief. Some of the recent competition has been supplied by other religions, but most of it comes from life philosophies that are distrustful, skeptical, or hateful of religious faith altogether. Many people today assume without question that religion is an expression of primitive consciousness, that the institution of Christianity is one of greed and superstition we would all be better off without. Today the Christian faith fights for its position in Western culture. In many areas it shows remarkable resiliency. In others, like northern Europe, it has been pronounced more or less "dead."

Some believers, their backs to the wall, now argue that "secularization" is actually the direct result of Christian teachings and world-view, so that the whole process is really a kind of oblique victory for the church. Their reasoning is at least partly persuasive. Christianity has tended to be an ideology of the world, so we shouldn't be surprised if the world is what we end up with. But what's hard to understand is why any Christian would take pleasure, or even consolation, in this. We aren't called to be of this world. Why do we struggle for a market share in it? Jesus says that the form of this world is passing away. Why then are we pleased to call that form our own?

The secularists are right. Christianity is a human institution; some day it will be no more. But they're wrong in assuming as a matter of fact that nothing endures, that everything is transitory. Of course, if all your investment is in finite objects and ideas, you can't imagine the presence of a transcendent reality. Only a people of faith can do that. This is a rare gift in an increasingly self-referential world, and one that still has the power to rock its foundations. But even this gift is useless if Christians won't use it to discriminate between what is finite and what is infinite, if they can't let go of what will die and hold fast to what cannot.

The only part of any faith that will last is the truth of its message, and only then if that message is an infinite one. The life and teachings of Jesus of Nazareth comprise the one unique and eternal element of our religion. And ironically, in our struggle to remain a powerful and prominent ideology of the world, we have abandoned them. That chief cornerstone has become the same stone which our builders rejected. Then, when rains come and winds blow, we wonder why our house falls so quickly. We just couldn't see it coming. Jesus warned us, but he's the last man we're prepared to hear.

◆   ◆   ◆

I once read about two Christian missionaries who spent a summer traveling in the backwoods of South Carolina. In their wanderings they came upon a Baptist church run by an elderly white preacher. The missionaries spoke only for a minute with this energetic old man, but found him to be quite a curiosity, and decided to look into his ministry a little further. So the next Wednesday night they snuck in the back of his country church. There they found a small but lively congregation of poor blacks and whites, standing and singing and worshipping side by side. The two sat quietly through the whole service, astonished by what they saw.

Afterwards they again approached the preacher and asked how such an unusual arrangement had come about in the segregated area where he lived. The old man said the answer was simple: one day he really started to read those gospels he had been talking about for so long. And they said that you should love all people, and share everything you have with them. So he started to preach that. It even seemed to him that that meant colored people too. So he started to preach *that*. What happened, he was asked? Well sir, he replied, I preached this church down to ten or twelve folk. How did your deacons take that? I fired them deacons, he said. It's my church. When your deacons don't *deak*, you got to fire them. The missionaries were simply stunned. Before them sat the old man, ornery and selfish and ignorant, amid his most motley flock. Not a large group, but faithful. It must have been a sight — black and white, young and old, sitting together and listening to their country parson teach a new thing, the gospel they'd never heard before.

For reasons we'll never understand, the Infinite embraces the powerless and the poor. But, stranger still, it embraces the selfish and the ignorant. This God uses not just what's available, but what seems to us least likely. Again, Simon Peter is our model. Peter was an effective and compelling witness to the gospel he had often betrayed. His strength was somehow made perfect in weakness. A man dumb as a rock provided solid enough a foundation. That little speck of what is perfect, that hint of the infinite, shines through the hazy casement of the finite and illumines it. And so Peter's Church performs the work of perfection in spite of the myriad imperfections that outnumber it.

Jesus doesn't choose Peter because he is unique. He chooses him because he's typical, a man of the usual human strengths and failings. Peter is an emblem of us all. Like him, we're ignorant and selfish and faithless. Like him, when our lives are threatened by the demands of the gospel, we deny it, as many times as it takes. And so, like him, we need to realize how complete our denial is, how far we stand from the values of the Nazarene. Like Peter, we need to hear a rooster crow. Peter died to himself in that awful moment. But because of that death he could then be reborn, forgiven in that strange seaside encounter at the end of the last gospel. The risen Christ turns to Peter and says, "Simon, son of John, do you love me more than these?" (Jesus never says what "these" are; we get the idea.) Yes Lord, says Peter. Jesus asks him the same question again. Yes Lord, Peter repeats. And a third time he asks him: "Simon, son of John, do you love me?" Peter is troubled and confused by this persistence, and says "Lord, you *know* I love you." Of course Jesus does. But standing beside a charcoal fire Peter had once denied him three times. And here, beside another charcoal fire, and a quiet breakfast of bread and fish, Jesus gives his most faithless and ignorant disciple the chance to affirm him three times. Jesus' final words to his friend? "Follow me."

It could be that the teachings of Jesus of Nazareth are just not for us. We may need something more common-sensical, more immediately useful, something more in accord with our nature and traditions. Maybe our in-born values are the ones we preferred all along, and we can learn to embrace them without the stamp of the "holy." Maybe the service of self is what we're most comfortable with. If this is true, it's a good thing to discover about ourselves, and the sooner the better. Because with that realization we would hear a rooster crow. We would feel the shock of eternity, see Jesus killed and buried, and finally confront the choices we make in denying him. We would search our hearts, and find nothing but ourselves: empty vessels, yes, but ready at last to be filled.

It was in Capernaum that Jesus first taught his followers they must eat the flesh and drink the blood of the Son of Man. One more crazy idea — Jesus himself asked "Do you take offense at this?" That was no way to win a following. But Jesus said it anyway, and at that moment "many drew back and no longer went about with him." Peter must have considered this too. At hearing such a scandalous teaching surely he was thrown back on himself for a moment. Could this really be the plan of an infinite God? And even if it is, could I bear to follow him? He, and all the disciples, found themselves at a crossroads. It was time to make a decision, and they knew it. So Jesus asked the twelve, straight out: "Will you also go away?" And what sad Peter said will be, in our emptiness, our answer too.

"Lord, to whom shall we go?"

SCRIPTURE REFERENCES

Translations taken from the Revised Standard, New International,
New Jerusalem, and King James Bibles

Foreword

Sufficient unto the day are the troubles thereof	Mt 6:34
No one has ever spoken like this man	Jn 7:46
... a new commandment...	Jn 13:34
... things hidden since the foundation of the world	Mt 13:35
[the kingdom]... has indeed caught you unawares	Mt 12:28
What is this? A new teaching!	Mk 1:27
... his own brothers did not believe in him	Jn 7:5
... they took offense at him	Mt 13:57
Where did he get all of this?	Mt 13:54
A prophet is not without honor...	Mk 6:4
... terror and anguish	Mk 14:34
... that neither toil nor spin	Mt 6:28
Suffer the little children...	Mk 10:14

Chapter One

... many have undertaken to compile a narrative...	Lk 1:1
... anyone who blasphemes against the Holy Spirit...	Mk 3:29
Why do you not understand what I say?	Jn 8:43
Blessed... who take no offense at me	Lk 7:23
As Jonah was to the Ninevites...	Lk 11:30
Let these words sink into your ears	Mt 13:9
... hate father and mother...	Lk 14:26
I tell you, these words of scripture are destined...	Lk 22:37
He has a demon	Jn 10:20
This is a hard saying...	Jn 6:60
... out of their own means	Lk 8:3

oppressed... who hunger and thirst...	Mt 5:6
Son of David...	Mt 15:22
... the lost sheep of the House of Israel	Mt 15:24
... take the children's food and throw it to the dogs	Mt 15:26
Ah yes, Lord, but even the dogs...	Mt 15:27
... a man's foes will be those of his own household	Mt 10:36
Your father and I have been looking for you...	Lk 2:48
Who are my mother and my brothers?	Mk 3:33
... his own brothers did not believe in him	Jn 7:5
... the son of Mary...	Mk 6:3
We were not born of fornication	Jn 8:41
... mother...	Jn 19:27
Woman, what have you to do with me?	Jn 2:4
Blessed is the womb that bore you...	Lk 11:27
Blessed rather are those who hear the word...	Lk 11:28
Do whatever he says	Jn 2:5

Chapter Two

the commandments of God... the precepts of men	Mk 7:8
Heaven and earth will pass away...	Mt 24:35
Continue in my word	Jn 8:31
... strain a gnat and swallow a camel	Mt 23:24
You will indeed listen, but never understand...	Mt 13:15
... would speak... only in parables	Mt 13:34
... Sons of Thunder...	Mk 3:17
Doubtless you will quote me the proverb...	Lk 4:23
... make disciples of all nations...	Mt 28:19
A sower sowed his seed...	Mt 13:3
Take care how you listen...	Lk 8:18
... become as a little child	Mk 10:15
... hidden from the learned... revealed to children	Mt 11:25
... have never seen are more blessed...	Jn 20:29
Those who are of the spirit are like the wind	Jn 3:8
... pore over the scriptures, believing that in them...	Jn 5:39
... born again	Jn 3:3
What is the kingdom of heaven like?	Lk 13:18
Lord, how can a man crawl back...	Jn 3:4

Chapter Three

Look, Teacher! What massive stones!	Mk 13:1
... fire from heaven...	Lk 9:54
The Son of Man came not to destroy the world...	Jn 12:47
... no sign to this evil generation...	Lk 11:29
... the Queen of the South	Mt 12:42
... haven't seen...	Jn 20:29
Do not rejoice that the spirits submit to you...	Lk 10:20
Listen! At the door are the footsteps...	Acts 5:9
... tested the spirit of the Lord...	Acts 5:9
... a great fear came upon the whole church	Acts 5:11

Chapter Four

Who... people say that I am	Lk 9:18
How long will you keep us in suspense?	Jn 10:24
... prophet like one of the prophets of old	Mk 6:15
... he has never studied	Jn 7:15
The kingdom of the heaven is at hand	Mt 3:2
... John, whose head I cut off...	Mk 6:16
... more than a prophet	Mt 11:9
Rabbi... a teacher come from God...	Jn 3:2
do whatever they tell you...	Mt 23:3
... the rabble, who know nothing of the law	Jn 7:49
... the poor in spirit...	Mt 5:3
They are damned	Jn 7:49
He had compassion on them...	Mk 6:34
... who think their gods will hear them...	Mt 6:7
... with authority...	Mk 1:27
... not be anxious about tomorrow	Mt 6:34
... salt of the earth	Mt 5:13
... the meek... hunger and thirst for righteousness	Mt 5:3-10
Do we pay taxes to Caesar or not?	Lk 20:22
Whose head is this?	Lk 20:24
... took them by surprise	Lk 20:26
Where your treasure is, there will your heart be also	Lk 12:34
... like to walk about in long robes...	Lk 20:46
... if someone swears by the Temple it is nothing...	Mt 23:16
What is highly esteemed in human eyes...	Lk 16:15

Chapter Five

How can you believe since you look to one another...   Jn 5:44
... precepts of men   Jn 8:15
... love human glory more than the glory of God   Jn 5:44
If someone should come in his own name...   Jn 5:43
... who gave [him] authority to act like this?   Mk 11:28
Who can forgive sins but God alone?   Mk 2:7
... that such powers were given to human beings   Mt 9:8
... calls God his own Father...   Jn 5:18
You will see heaven opened...   Jn 1:51
... greater than the Temple...   Mt 12:6
Is it not written in your Law: 'I said...'   Jn 10:34

Chapter Six

... who loved money...   Lk 16:14
... a tainted thing...   Lk 16:11
... to give than to receive   Acts 20:35
A man's life does not consist in the abundance...   Lk 12:15
... the things of this world...   Lk 12:30
You cannot be the slave both of God and money   Lk 16:13
... the lure of riches...   Mk 4:19
The poor you will always have with you   Jn 12:8
Blessed are you who are poor...   Lk 6:20
... good measure, pressed down, shaken together...   Lk 6:38

Chapter Seven

I have overcome the world   Jn 16:33
... keep away from these men and let them alone...   Acts 5:38
... held in high regard by the people...   Acts 5:34
... the Father, who sees in secret, will reward you   Mt 6:4
... judge according to the flesh   Jn 8:15
... the ruler of this world...   Jn 16:11
You will either love the first and hate the second...   Lk 16:13
... rulers lord it over them...   Lk 22:25
... the one who rules is like the one who serves   Lk 22:26
Human glory means nothing to me   Jn 5:41

Every plant which my heavenly Father...   Mt 15:13
... not my will, but yours...   Lk 22:42
It has been handed over to me to give to anyone...   Lk 4:6
You are not on the side of God, but of men   Mk 8:33
... a scandal to Jews and foolishness to Gentiles   1 Cor 1:23
Do you still not understand?   Mk 8:17
If any want to become my followers...   Mk 8:34
He is beside himself   Mk 3:21
... look to one another for approval   Jn 5:44

Chapter Eight

... an eye for an eye...   Deut 19:21
God is kind to the ungrateful and selfish...   Lk 6:35
... causes the sun to rise on the bad...   Mt 5:45
... the Tower of Siloam fell...   Lk 13:4
... blind guides... children of Hell...   Mt 23:15
You clean the outside of cup and dish...   Mt 23:25
You are those who justify yourselves before others   Lk 16:15
Did not Moses give you the law?   Jn 7:19
It is Moses who accuses you, the very Moses...   Jn 5:45
You shut up the kingdom of heaven in people's faces   Mt 23:13
If you were blind you would have no guilt...   Jn 9:41
The standard you use will be used for you...   Mt 7:2
We have a law, and by that law he ought to die   Jn 19:7
Behold, the days are coming, says the Lord...   Jer 31:31-4
... the greatest commandment of the Law...   Mt 22:36
... first...   Mk 12:28
How do you read it?   Lk 10:26
And who is my neighbor?   Lk 10:29
... half dead...   Lk 10:30
Learn what it means, 'I desire mercy...   Mt 9:13
Why don't you judge for yourselves what is right?   Lk 12:57
Every teacher of the law who has been instructed...   Mt 13:52
Nothing will be impossible for you   Mt 17:20
Be of good cheer. I have overcome the world   Jn 16:33
... bear false witness...   Ex 20:16
Wise as serpents... harmless as doves   Mt 10:16

You have heard it said, 'And eye for an eye'...	Mt 5:38-9
You have heard it said, 'Love your neighbor'...	Mt 5:43-4
Up to the time of John it was the Law...	Mt 11:12
A new commandment I give you...	Jn 13:34
Love others as I have loved you	Jn 13:34
... do good to those who hate you...	Lk 6:27-8
It is not those who say to me 'Lord, Lord'...	Mt 7:21
Everyone will know you are my disciples...	Jn 13:35
... mother and brothers...	Lk 8:21
... do not practice what they preach...	Mt 23:3
Why do you keep calling me 'Lord, Lord' and...	Lk 6:46
... a stupid man who built his house on sand...	Mt 7:26
What a fall it had!	Mt 7:27

Afterword

Simon, son of John, do you love me more than these?	Jn 21:15
Follow me	Jn 21:19
Do you take offense at this?	Jn 6:61
Lord, to whom shall we go?	Jn 6:68

So then, as you received Jesus as Lord and Christ, now live your lives in him and built up on him, held firm by the faith that you have been taught, and overflowing with thanksgiving. Make sure that no one captivates you with the empty lure of a "philosophy" of the kind that human beings hand on, based on the principles of this world and not on Christ.... He has wiped out the record of your debt to the Law, which stood against us; he has destroyed it by nailing it to the cross; and he has stripped the sovereignties and the ruling forces, and paraded them in public, behind him in his triumphal procession.

Then never let anyone criticize you for what you eat and drink, or about observance of annual festivals, New Moons or Sabbaths. These are only a shadow of what was coming: the reality is the body of Christ. Do not be cheated of your prize by anyone who chooses to grovel to angels and worship them, pinning every hope on visions received, vainly puffed up by a human way of thinking; such a person has no connection to the Head, by which the whole body, given all that it needs and held together by its joints and sinews, grows with the growth given by God.

If you have really died with Christ to the principles of this world, why do you still let rules dictate to you, as though you were still living in the world? — 'Do not pick this up, do not eat that, do not touch the other,' and all about things which perish even while they are being used — according to merely human commandments and doctrines! In these rules you can indeed find what seems to be good sense — the cultivation of the will, and a humility which takes no account of the body; but in fact they have no value against self-indulgence.

Since you have been raised up to be with Christ, you must look for the things that are above, where Christ is, sitting at God's right hand. Let your thoughts be on things above, not on the things that are on the earth, because you have died, and now the life you have is hidden with Christ in God.

Colossians 2:6 - 3:3